A Collection of Uzbek Short Stories

A Collection of Uzbek Short Stories

Translated by
Mahmuda Saydumarova

authorHOUSE®

Bloomington, IN, U.S.A.

AuthorHouse™
1663 Liberty Drive
Bloomington, IN 47403
www.authorhouse.com
Phone: 1-800-839-8640

Published by AuthorHouse   12/20/2012

ISBN: 978-1-4772-9722-3 (sc)
ISBN: 978-1-4772-9721-6 (hc)
ISBN: 978-1-4772-9723-0 (e)

Library of Congress Control Number: 2012923199

Table of Contents

Preface.. vii

How Sweet You are, You Bitter Life! 1
My Thief Boy...18
The Literature Teacher 25
The Brides' Revolution 30
The Bride from the City 42
The Grandfather and his Grandson 56
The Rainbow..62
Ramazon 73
The Sensitive Case...76
How I was a "Mister" for a Month! 81

Biographical Information..91

Preface

Uzbekistan, located in Central Asia, is a relatively young country that appeared on the map after the end of the Soviet Union in 1991. In the present day, its population consists of approximately 30 million people. The Uzbek people live in all the neighboring countries of Uzbekistan as well. Uzbek literature has a history which goes back more than a thousand years.

Having translated this collection of ten short stories from Modern Uzbek Literature to English to bring into the American reader's attention, I would like to briefly mention a few words about the genre of short story in Uzbek literature.

The literature of this era is an embodiment of the best samples chosen from a thousand-year history literature. It is also a realistic literature which reveals the social and political events that take place in real life. For this collection, I have tried my best to include various stories that pertain to the Uzbek nation's cultural life of different periods.

In Khayriddin Sultonov's "How Sweet You Are, You Bitter Life!", an elderly woman, Qurbonjon dodkhoh, who is the head of the opposition movement fighting against the invaders, is able to bid farewell to her son, who is held captive by the neighboring Russian general invader. This is described in moving detail. She comes to her son just before he is about to be hanged by Kaufman's orders and states, "Farewell, my son. Your father and grandfather have also martyred at the hands of their enemies; we have inherited martyrdom. I am satisfied with what I have fed you."

The story, "My Thief Boy," narrates the devastating events that took place in the year 1917 with disturbing realism. Late in the evening, an interesting conversation starts between a thief, lying on top of the roof and an old woman, lying next to her sleeping grandchildren. The thief is not actually a thief but has become one because of life's difficulties trying to earn a living to support his family. On the other hand, the old woman is a helpless grandmother who spends the nights worrying about the fate of her orphan grandchildren. Both of them have their own pains and sorrows. As a result, they engage in a heartfelt conversation, listening to each other's woes. Their conversation is so natural and so realistic that both characters become a permanent memory in the reader's mind.

Abdulla Qahhor, who is also referred to as the Uzbek literature's Chekhov, has made a great contribution to the development of the Uzbek short story. There is a kind of sarcasm waiting to be revealed in Qahhor's satirical stories of this era. Boqijon Boqayev in "The Literature Teacher" is one example of a satirical character who has been confronted by this kind of sarcasm. Even though he is ostensibly a literature teacher, he is unable to answer his sister-in-law's simple questions and changes the subject every chance he gets. By so doing, he disgraces himself and reveals that he is in fact a simpleton.

Another story I have chosen for this collection is Said Ahmad's "The Bride's Revolution." This story is considered to be one of the representative stories portraying Uzbek customs and traditions as well as the mother-in-law and daughter-in-law relationship in Uzbek society. A play, which has been created on the basis of this story, has been shown in theaters for several years. Another story related to this topic is a young writer, Nargiza Ghulomova's "The Bride from the City," which was written during Uzbekistan's period of independence.

Oydin Hojiyeva's "Ramazon" and Normurod Norqobulov's "The Rainbow" are stories related to children's literature. As for Toghay Murod's "The Grandfather and his Grandson," it describes the relationship between the older generation and young children; it also describes how the surrounding environment is viewed from two different viewpoints.

Farhod Musajonov's "The Sensitive Case" is a story written in the genre of comedy. Similarly, in "How I was a 'Mister' for a Month!" Sa'dulla Siyoyev expresses his pride of the Uzbek nation by illustrating Uzbek customs and traditions and some facts related to the Uzbek history through his interaction with an American tourist and his letters to him.

I hope that these short stories will give an idea, albeit somewhat brief, of Uzbekistan and the Uzbek society to the American reader.

How Sweet You are, You Bitter Life!

by Khayriddin Sultonov

From 1865 to 1880, Qurbonjon dodkhoh, the Queen of Oloy, gathered the nation around her, and with a single sword in her hand, fought against General Fon Kaufman. She was so courageous that when her son, Qamchibek, was held as a captive by Kaufman and was about to be hanged by his orders, she came to the gallows and told her son, "Farewell, my son. Your father and grandfather have also martyred at the hands of their enemies; we have inherited martyrdom. I am satisfied with what I have fed you." Saying this, she turned around, climbed her horse, and without watching her son die in torture and pain, left.

Ghafur Ghulom

*   *   *

Eighteen seventy-six, the twenty-sixth of February. Marghilan.

This chilly, gloomy winter day that resembled any other wintry day was almost over. As usual, the voices of the callers to prayer woke up the city at the crack of dawn. And as usual, after hurriedly performing ablution[1] while shivering in the cold, the Muslims headed

---

[1]   ablution: the act of washing oneself as part of a religious rite

1

to the mosque. As they walked on the pavement, the sound of their boots walking on the freshly-fallen snow could be heard. Also, as usual, there was a thin, bluish fog hanging on top of the high and low roofs. Today also, even the sun that looked like a worn-out coin shone its rays for just a little while and, as if feeling cold, hid itself under thick, gray clouds. And as usual, the people of the city scattered in the empty streets, with the hope of trying to make a living, and somehow livened the bleak and gloomy city.

In short, in this quiet, depressing day that seemed to be drowning in poverty just like the thousands of days that the city had witnessed, all of a sudden, a distinctive hubbub arose. Coming from all four directions, a huge crowd of people soon filled the yard of the marketplace. Ever since it was built, the city had not witnessed such a crowd before. The unmerciful cold slapped people's faces and eyes and pierced into their very bones like a pricking needle; it smacked the icicles hanging from the rainspouts with its whip and chased away all living beings into their nests. It roared the crowd that had assembled at the wide yard, next to the horse market. Among the crowd were shop-keepers who had closed their shops hurriedly in fear of the Russian mustached-soldiers with unmerciful eyes, women who had left their warm homes and did not understand why they had come here, old women who ceaselessly muttered 'There is no might nor power except with God,' scowling old men with open chests, and children who were about to start crying and whose snots were flowing down their noses.

"Qamchibek will be hanged!" These were the only words that were uttered over and over from everybody's lips. There was terror hanging in everybody's hearts.

Cossacks besieged the yard in a circular shape. General Fon Kaufman—the governor of Turkistan, Major General Trotsky—the head of the penalty delegation who had white hair and black eyes and eyebrows, the good-looking, well-behaved Prince Boyarskiy, the crippled Colonel Lusarov, other important people from the military administration in Fergana region, as well as civil servants who were shivering either from the cold or from fear took their places one after another on a wooden platform that was temporarily put up.

The wind started blowing even stronger. More Russian soldiers marched into the yard and formed a square shape, according to the orders of an officer who was standing at the head of the line. The officer, who was called Major Lyahov, neared the platform and gave a military greeting to Kaufman and said, "Everything is ready, your highness. Permission to start?"

Kaufman looked at his watch and said, "One minute, major. My wife also wanted to attend; let us wait for awhile. Oh, there she is."

A blue carriage drawn by two horses entered the yard. One of the assistants who were standing near the platform hurried over to the carriage and opened the door. Two women wearing expensive leather coats with fur collars and carefully lifting their blue dresses under their coats got out. One of them was somewhat old, yet her good-looking appearance hid this. Saying something to her friend, she headed to the platform and as she did so, Fon Kaufman also took some steps towards her. His assistants followed him, with a smile on their faces.

"Oh, forgive me, my dear, for we are a bit late. Don't get angry. You know how we women are; the mirror is such a magnet," the woman walking in front said. As she smiled to the officers, she gently said to them, "Hello, young men."

Trotsky, Lusarov, Lyahov, and Prince Boyraskiy approached her one by one and kissed her thin fingers as white as snow.

"Oh Prince!" Kaufman's wife addressed Prince Boyarskiy, shaking her head. "You completely forgot us, prince; this isn't something good, for God's sake, it's not good. Our stay has almost come to an end, soon . . . Oh, get introduced, this lady is Countess Anna Ippolitovna, Colonel Sherbakov's wife. Do you say, 'We know each other'? Oh prince, prince!"

The general's assistant stood smiling.

The governor's wife looked at Lusarov and said, "I do not long at all for frightening scenes as this. Yesterday I asked my husband, 'Who are the ones who caused the rebellion?' and he told me, 'If you attend tomorrow, you'll see.' Tell me please, colonel, are they terrifying to this extent?" Lusarov smiled without opening his mouth; he started talking about something in a serious tone. It was obvious that although the governor's wife seemed to be listening to Lusarov, she was actually thinking about something else.

"Begin!" Kaufman ordered to Lyahov. "Bring him out!"

A thick-bearded old soldier, wearing red boots took off his military coat, adjusted the chair under the gallows, checked the rope

4

meticulously, wiped the snow off his boots, and headed towards the other side of the yard. An uproar arose among the crowd; four muscular Cossacks brought in a young man wearing a torn coat. His hands were tied and marks of torture and blood were visible on his face.

"Is this him?" asked Countess Sherbakova, opening her beautiful blue eyes very wide. "Yes, countess," answered Boyarskiy. "Poor thing!" pitied Countess Sherbakova.

"Oh, monsieur, I don't think I can handle this," the governor's wife said, with a sigh. "It has become cold, hasn't it?"

"It would be better if you went home, dear," Kaufman said. "You might catch a cold. Yesterday, you said that you had a headache. And anyway, this isn't Saint Petersburg."

"It's alright; I want to stay for a little longer," the governor's wife whispered.

Colonel Lusarov gave the paper in his hand to Lyahov who had just got on the stage. The major stepped forward and started reading the verdict in a loud and clear voice:

"The military court at the military department in Fergana region has looked at the case of the suspect, Qamchibek bin Olimbek, a local of the Uzbek nation and it consists of his criminal act against the sultanate of the royal emperor. And on the basis of overwhelming evidence and many witnesses of which Abdulrahman is one, it has been justified that he is a very harmful person. He has caused physical harms to the royal emperor, his sultanate, and the military system. The suspect Qamchibek bin Olimbek along with his brothers, Abdullahbek, Mahmudbek, and Hasanbek, who are the leaders of the armed groups, have caused several disturbances in Oloy Valley and have lead the local residents to go against the system which had been set up by the military administration's Governor General. During the past three years, his murderous gangsters, who are the country's criminals have caused physical harm to the army, the human force, and the nutrition sources. Several warnings have been directed to Qamchibek bin Olimbek but he has ignored them. The result of active violence and aggression of these savage groups that went on for eight years . . ."

A short officer approached the platform from the back and whispered something in Colonel Lusarov's ear. Lusarov's face whitened. "Your highness," he whispered to Kaufman hurriedly, "your highness, Qurbonjon dodkhoh is coming!"

Kaufman immediately looked at him, "How is that? Aren't there any guards assigned on the way?"

"There are, your highness. Prince Boyarskiy and his soldiers are guarding the gates and main entrances; however, dodkhoh is coming all alone!"

"What?"

"It's true, your highness."

"Then, she *is* in the city. I cannot understand this. Has this woman lost her senses? Doesn't she know that fifteen thousand soms[2] have been announced as a reward for her head?"

"Alright, colonel," Kaufman continued, after calming down. "Go on, let us see how things play out."

"So, should I give an order to imprison her?"

"Why? An old, helpless, disarmed woman, in the daylight in front of everyone at the city's yard. No, colonel, only make sure that she is observed. Perhaps she wants to bid farewell to her son. Why should we deprive her from her rights? Be a bit humane, colonel."

"As you wish, your highness."

". . . The military court at the military department in Fergana region has looked at the case of the suspect, Qamchibek bin Olimbek, a local of the Uzbek nation and his criminal act against the emperor's sultanate. The court has released a verdict to hang him; the verdict is final and no complaints will be accepted. The General Governor Fon Kaufman—the head of the military court, New Marghilan. 1876, 26th February."

Major Lyahov completed reading the verdict and looking in the direction of Kaufman, nodded his head. The Cossacks brought Qamchibek under the gallows. Kaufman called for Sibgatullin, the interpreter wearing the clothes of a sergeant.

---

2   som: Uzbek currency

"Ask the suspect if he has any final words." Kaufman asked him.

The translator did not have a chance to ask; his voice drowned in an uproar that suddenly arose. Qurbonjon dodkhoh was riding her horse and approaching quickly; she was wearing a blue, velvet traditional suit and on her head was a cotton shawl. Between the crowd and Qurbonjon dodkhoh was a distance of thirty feet. On everyone's faces were confusion, wonder, hesitation, and fear.

"Colonel!" Kaufman gave a signal to Colonel Lusarov with a white-gloved hand. "There, look now, dodkhoh is coming fearlessly. It wouldn't be bad if your soldiers would take this woman's bravery as a role model. A displaced bullet from any corner might kill her, am I right?" Lusarov stared at him.

"Just look at her, she doesn't look the least bit scared!" Kaufman said, smiling. "But a displaced bullet is a displaced bullet. What do you think, Lusarov?"

"I understand, your highness," Lusarov whispered. "There is a hunter in my squad. Yepifanov, a soldier."

"Very well, colonel. Make sure that dodkhoh leaves the yard safe and sound. The displaced bullet might hit her from any corner; did you understand?"

"I understand, your highness."

The translator muttered his question for the third time, but Qamchibek did not respond. He looked towards his mother; his eyes were filled with grief, pain, and longing. "Mother! My dear mother!" he screamed in a loud voice.

The rider approached with beautiful strength; her horse strided with steady steps. Dodkhoh's face reflected silence and sublime tranquility, as if she was completely blind to her son being about to be killed and as if she could not hear his painful murmurings. She proudly approached with her white-haired head held high.

The audience stirred like the waves of the ocean and angrily roared. Even the soldiers and officers froze in amazement, not one soul knew what to say or what to do. Even General Kaufman froze in his place, like a statue. Dodkhoh neared the Russian soldiers' ring and pulled up her horse about five feet away from them. There was a heavy silence, as heavy and as rigid as a stone.

"My son!" dodkhoh said. Her voice trembled for a while; however, she then spoke in a coercing, heroic tone. "My son, we have inherited martyrdom, for your father and grandfather have both martyred at the hands of their enemies. Farewell, my son. I'm contented with what I have fed you," Qurbonjon dodkhoh said these words, got on her steed, and hit it with her whip. The horse jumped, lifted up its rider, and hurried away.

"Be satisfied with me, mother!" Qamchibek said. "Be satisfied with me!"

"I'm satisfied a thousand times," Dodkhoh said and opened her hands for prayer. "We will meet at the Day of Judgment." Then she turned and hurried away with her horse to the east. Two hot tears dropped on the horse's hair, and these two drops burned the horse's whole existence.

Chaos increased among the audience. Kaufman fell into deep thinking and said to himself, "Yes, astonishing!"

"So, is she the one they call the 'Queen of Oloy'?" asked his wife. "But they used to say that she is a very old woman!? However, this lady rides a horse with such ease. Tell me, dear, why didn't they catch her?"

"There is no need to," Kaufman said, smiling. "She . . . will give up herself. I will force her to do that!"

"Listen to me, monsieur, I know you do not like those who mind your business, but could you just not kill this young man?" Kaufman's wife said, fixing the collar of her coat. "He is very young, it's such a pity. Of course, I'm not saying that he should be left without any punishment. But isn't there any other way? For example, sending him to Siberia for hard labor?"

"No!" said Kaufman and again repeated in a stern voice, "No! You heard the verdict. No mercy is shown towards an enemy, never! Lusarov!"

"Yes, your highness?"

"Speed it up!"

"Very well."

"Who is that soldier? Is it Yepifanov?"

"Yes, your highness, it's Yepifanov!"

"Alright."

Lusarov looked at Lyahov and gave him a sign; Lyahov waved the handkerchief in his hand and moved backwards. Drums were played. Two strong, tall Cossacks placed a rope round Qamchibek's neck. A coatless, old soldier, wearing a black mask that covered his face and eyes got on his knees and prayed; then he stretched his hand toward the rope.

"Oh God!" Countess Sherbakova's face whitened and she took hold of Prince Boyarskiy's hand with her cold fingers. "Oh God! How terrifying this scene is!"

"Don't be scared, countess, don't be scared. This takes only one moment," Prince Boyarskiy said, holding her from her arm.

"Ach, mein Gott, das is schlecht! Ach, mein Gott!" the governor's wife said and immediately closed her eyes.

As Qamchibek's feet moved away from the ground, he kept repeating, "There is no God but Allah." The audience suddenly stirred and someone screamed. The black-masked soldier kicked away the chair under Qamchibek's feet with force. The young, strong body swung for awhile, hanging from the rope and suddenly fell on the ground. Lyahov was puzzled; he drew out his sword, hurried over to the gallows, and froze over the suspect. Kaufman looked at Lusarov with fuming eyes. People started talking in loud voices:

"Oh God, this is from your power!"

"What happened? What happened?"

"God didn't like . . ."

"Gentlemen, what are you looking at?"

"Hey you, move out of my way!"

"No, you move, idiot!"

Trotsky's loud voice was heard from among the crowd's voices. "Silence! Be quiet or else I'll shoot you all! Silence!" The soldiers adjusted their artilleries as if believing his words. A young man's shrilling, nervous voice covered Trotsky's voice, "Is there any man wearing any belt in here?"

Kaufman looked at Lusarov with furious eyes, "Lusarov! What is the meaning of this?"

"Your highness . . ."

"I said what is the meaning of this?"

"Allow me to explain, your highness . . ."

"Enough! This is disgrace! Betrayal!"

"Forgive me, your highness, it is a coincidence . . ."

"Coincidence? You say coincidence? You can be hanged yourself right now, but I assure you, *that* will not be a coincidence! This is disgrace! Go!"

"What happened? Oh, tell me, what happened? Look at me, prince, what happened?" the governor's wife asked, looking around her in confusion.

Boyarskiy was disgusted. "The rope got torn apart! What else would happen?"

"Oh, there now, I told you so. Don't you see? Even God does not want him to die!" the governor's wife said, looking at her husband.

"You look tired, my dear," said Kaufman. "It would be better if you went home. Prince, please escort these ladies."

"No, no! We will not leave until we see this until the end, am I right, Anna Ippolitovna?" The countess, whose color had turned white as snow, wiped her cheeks and eyes with her handkerchief.

Qamchibek was still lying unconscious under the rope. One of the soldiers started scrubbing snow on his face; he opened his eyes. Looking around and feeling dizzy, Qamchibek tried to stand up and wiped the blood that was dripping down from the corner of his lips that had turned blue.

"It's an old rope," he shivered. He got up from the ground and proudly shouted, "It's an old rope!" The old soldier's face showed fear and anger. He once again placed the rope round his neck with trembling fingers. The drums were played and it was as if the earth and skies were shaking. Qamchibek gulped. He took deep breaths. Pearls of sweat appeared on his forehead. The final breath!

The final moment!

The final torture!

How sweet you are, you bitter life!

There were white clouds swimming in the sky. The gentle breeze blowing from the Aravon Mountains brought with it its last scent filled with uncertain hopes. Then, there were neither breeze, nor clouds, nor skies.

Kaufman got down from the platform and he stood for awhile to bid goodbye to his wife. The countess, wearing gloves that covered her hands and arms, ceaselessly kept mumbling, "Oh, what a pity! He's a human being, a human being!" Then she looked at Boyarskiy and added, "Alright, farewell prince. By the way, tell me, you will come to our house tonight to play cards with us, won't you? Please do come, we will be waiting for you. Forgive us, prince, this game is the only source of entertainment we have in here. I suppose, in this wild country, we ourselves will soon become wild. No music, no theater. I hope we will return back to Tashkent soon. So, we will wait for you tonight. You will get to know Countess Sherbakova. You're a grave person, prince. Alright then, au revoir, monsieur!"

The carriage started moving. Accompanied by the soldiers, Kaufman went towards the gate of the market. His assistant brought him a black, Turkmen horse, but he refused and shook his head. He turned to a narrow alley at the end of the yard. Everyone was quiet. Lusarov, not taking his eyes off the ground, was also walking quietly. After walking a distance of about thirty feet, Kaufman looked at the colonel questioningly, "Colonel Lusarov?"

"Yes, your highness?"

"The soldier?"

"Yes, your highness, after turning this corner, now . . ."

Fifteen feet away from the narrow alley's corner, Soldier Yepifanov's tall body could be seen; he was walking solemnly. As soon as he saw his masters, he froze in his place.

"Well, Yepifanov?" Lusarov asked questioningly, as he approached him. Yepifanov's long beard shuddered, but he kept silent.

"Why are you silent, Yepifanov?" asked Kaufman in a gentle voice and put his hand on Yepifanov's broad shoulders.

"Your highness . . ." Yepifanov stammered, as if his tongue could not fit inside his mouth. "Your highness . . ."

"Didn't your bullet hit her?" Lusarov's eyes filled with blood. Yepifanov gripped his rifle so tightly that his fingernails started hurting. He said, "I could not shoot her, your highness." He moved his fat lips and whispered in a voice that was barely hearable, "I could not shoot . . ."

"Why couldn't you shoot, Yepifanov?" Kaufman's voice was still gentle.

"Your highness . . . for God's sake, forgive me, your highness . . ." Yepifanov looked at the governor pleadingly. "I don't know what happened, everything was clear from above that roof . . . but I couldn't, your highness, I remembered my mother . . ."

There was a heavy, nervous silence for a moment. Then Lusarov's brutal voice was heard, "To hell with your mother!" Cursing him, he savagely and furiously attacked Yepifanov.

Kaufman lifted his finger and stopped the colonel. He then approached Yepifanov and observed him from head to foot. He finally said in a loud voice, "Well done, Soldier Yepifanov. You did what a real soldier would have done." He put his hand on the confused soldier's shoulders. Kaufman turned around and quickly climbed on the horse that his assistant was holding. The horsemen left, leaving the soldier in the falling snow.

"Lusarov!" Kaufman said, getting down in front of the army's dwelling. "I believe that it is important to reward Soldier Yepifanov for his service. Did you understand?" He gave a certain meaningful look. "He must absolutely be rewarded!"

"I understand, your highness," Lusarov nodded his head.

Two months passed. One day, a drunk postman, who was barely able to sit in his carriage knocked on one of the huts in Gribovo village in Orlov region. He handed a piece of paper, which had traveled a distance of thousands of kilometers and was almost lost on the way, to an old woman wearing a black shawl. The old woman read the paper and immediately fell on the floor. The cold wind blowing in front of the hut blew open the letter:

". . . we inform you with pain and grief that your son, Yefim Yepifanov has been killed while serving the czar and his country.

The team's leader, Colonel Lusarov."

The wind blew strongly.

My Thief Boy

A Realistic Story
by Ghafur Ghulom

Several years have passed since our father's death. This year, in the spring of 1917, we lost our mother as well and so we became orphans. Our grandmother, our mother's mother, moved in to live with us and to take care of us. Her nickname was 'Black Grandmother,' and so we called her that.

All four of us sleep with our grandmother under a veranda, which is open from the front. We cover ourselves with old, worn-out blankets and under us is a single, dirty, worn rug.

One evening, towards the end of September and the beginning of fall, the weather was quite chilly. We four orphans were sleeping, snuggling with each other, and keeping one another warm. Our 'black grandmother' was lying down at the far end of the veranda, just like a mother bird. She is over eighty years old and she has a habit of smoking tobacco.

It was this night, after midnight when I woke up to disturbing sounds. My grandmother was talking with someone in a very loud voice. Our house is big and square in shape; we have inherited it from our grandfather. It is surrounded by big, tall houses from all four directions. Our cousins live to the north of us but during summers, they move to a garden house and for this reason, that part of the area is empty.

Imagine! A thief broke into our house! It seems that there are some people in the world who think of us as human beings!? I'll talk about this to my friends with pride tomorrow. "A thief broke into our house," I'll tell them, with my head high and feeling proud. But I wonder if they are going to believe me.

That thief had climbed the roof of our cousins' house and had slowly walked in our direction. But he must have sneezed when he reached here because my grandmother, who was hugging a pillow and deep in thought, with tobacco under her tongue, got disturbed by him. She spit out the tobacco, looked towards the roof, and said, "My thief boy! It seems to me that you have climbed the roof to steal something in order to provide for your family. But your job isn't easy; couldn't you at least have waited until you got rid of that cold?"

"Grandmother, don't you think it would be better for you to rest and sleep for one night? Or will you stop me from doing my job?" replied the thief.

I probably woke up when the conversation had reached here; I will write the rest of the conversation as I heard it.

"My thief boy, do you think that I can sleep when I have all these misfortunes to think about? It has been six months that I haven't slept a single hour. During the day, I walk around and I feel as if my head is like a spinning top, so I sit down somewhere and drowse off just like birds do. And during nights, I go deep into my own thoughts and imagination."

"What do you think about, grandmother?" asked the thief. Then, he took off his coat, folded it, lied down on his side, and used his coat as a pillow.

"I think about the future of these four orphans, my thief boy. What else would I think about? You can see that life is hard; it's harder than a rock. And it's even harder to earn a loaf of bread, even if it's the size of a camel's eye. It's very hard for these orphans' only uncle, who is a wagon driver, to provide for them because he has to take care of his own family. There is not a single thing left for us to see and touch in this house. We sell our things, one after another, and with that money, we buy our food. A mountain of money is never enough for spending, as they say. When will these little ones grow up and eat from their own earning? One has to think about this even if he does not want to. And to top all of this, only one of these orphans is a boy and he is the eldest. He is fourteen years old; he hasn't reached fifteen. The rest are girls; I wonder when these girls will find their own places in life. If there won't be anyone to take care of them and provide for them, then who will want them? Life is difficult, my thief boy, life is very difficult!"

"You speak the truth, grandmother," the thief said. "I also have a wife, two children, and my old mother to take care of. Like they say, a chicken needs both seeds and water to survive; so I have to provide for my family. I go through lots of difficulties and pain to earn four loaves of bread. I have strength in my arms and I'm mentally healthy if I want to work. Do you think that I like being a thief? I'm the son of a shoe-maker; my father has many children. Things have turned upside down. They said that the war would be over when Kerensky[3] became czar. However, it doesn't seem that the war will be over soon. Life is for the strong ones, until now."

"Can't you do some other profession, other than stealing, my boy?" asked my grandmother.

"What should I work as? All vocations are going through crisis. Should I make shoes, like my father? First of all, to make shoes, there is neither leather, nor glue, nor nails, nor paint. The materials cost thrice as much as the price of readymade shoes. And if I work as a porter, there aren't any rich people who buy grains and vegetables in big bags anymore. Several days ago, Buvamat, one of the most successful shoe-makers in our district, exchanged all his shoe-making tools for two pods of corn. What he did was right because there aren't any Uzbek, Kazakh, or Kirghiz farmers who wear the shoes that he makes anymore. Only their orphans are left, and they wander around in the city. There are several of these orphans who stretch out their hands and say, 'Uncle, please give me some bread.' They're in every corner that I look at, in every house that I enter, and they ask for bread. Yes, bread! I can't provide that even for my own children. It's not only me, but all shoe-makers are like that. All craftsmen, weavers, and even school teachers and scientists are in the same pitiful situation. All of them long for a spoonful of vegetable soup; all of them wander around."

---

[3] Kerensky: a king of the Russian government, who came into power after the caesarian system's upheaval in February, 1917

"May God curse the war! Maybe this is the end of the world, my thief boy; and maybe there is a blessing written for these orphans. Okay, let me ask you now; you have entered into this illegal path from desperateness. So why don't you rob rich people's houses? In this neighborhood, there is Karim Qori, the fabric seller, Odil Khojaboy, the contractor, Muhammad Yaquboy, the investor; and they have a lot of money and their houses are full. Even their little child eats from a plate etched with poetry. Why don't you go to their houses and make holes in their roofs?"

"You're naïve, grandma, you're naïve," said the thief. "Is it possible to get into rich people's houses, whose walls are high and whose doors are made of iron? Not to mention that each house is guarded by two or three dogs; which are as big as donkeys. If just a butterfly flies over their house, they bark for a whole week. Odil Khojaboy's house is guarded by a Russian guard who has a rifle; and I want to live! Even if I do not get killed, I might be sent to Siberia."

"You do have a point, my thief boy; just be careful. Do not get your reputation spoilt in front of people," my grandmother said.

"You're right, grandma. The other day, I stole four hens and a rooster from Orif's barn."

"Do you say that you stole a hen and a rooster? These creatures might crow, you know. Didn't you get caught?" my grandmother asked.

"Every problem has a solution," the thief replied. "I take a bottle of water with me whenever I go to steal chickens. I fill my mouth with water, I get closer to the chicken, and sprinkle water over it. Chickens are the most stupid creatures in the world. The chicken thinks it's raining and hides its head under its wing and stays quiet. As for me, I take the chickens from their necks, one by one, and put them in my bag."

"This is how it goes, then. So every profession has its own nuances," my grandmother said.

"But you know, grandma, I was about to get exposed. I gave a rooster to Rahmon Khoja; he is the mayor of our district and he closed up the case. Rahmon Khoja treats me well and he is a good man. Last year I bribed him and gave him eighty-three rubles, the money I had collected after selling a few things. I said to him, 'This is all that I have, mayor,' and so he excused me from going to rabochiy.[4]"

"May God bless him. Okay, my thief boy, dawn will approach after a little while. That bright star has already reached the peak. Get down from there from the tree near the kitchen. We haven't any firewood left. In the kitchen, there's a big trunk of the almond tree that used to be in our house long time ago. Take an axe and cut some firewood form this trunk for us. I'll make some tea; I had kept two small loaves that your uncle had given yesterday. We will have breakfast together."

---

[4]   rabochiy: a Russian word meaning 'worker.' During World War I, the Russian colonialist government used to collect men from the colonized Islamic republics and send them to Siberia as workers for hard labor.

"No, grandma, I could cut the firewood for you, but I won't drink tea with you because you'll know who I am when the sun goes up. I have a reputation that I don't want to lose."

"Oh my! Are you going to leave our holy house with nothing, my thief boy? Take something with you, hold on. Let's see what you can take . . . Oh yes, there's a big, old pot in the kitchen. Long time ago, there were many people in this house and we used to eat from this big pot. However, only these four orphans remain in this big house now. They're not going to cook anything in this big pot, so take it and sell it. You might need the money for something, my thief boy."

"No, grandmother, don't be so pessimistic. These days will go away quickly and we will forget them in the blink of an eye. Soon, there'll be a big family in here again and this big pot will seem small then. This belongs to the orphans so let them benefit from it. We're going to serve them in their weddings, God willing. Now I have to say goodbye and leave, grandma. The sun's already rising from behind the mountains."

"Goodbye, my thief boy. Visit us sometimes," my grandmother said.

"Okay, ma'am, okay," replied the thief and vanished from sight.

As for me, I know who the thief is but until now, I haven't revealed his identity to anyone!

The Literature Teacher

by Abdulla Qahhor

A literature teacher, Boqijon Boqayev, or—the teacher of the beautiful arts—as he called himself, entered the barn. He got angry because he found a tick in the cow's ear; but when he tried to remove the tick and the cow shook its head and snorted, he got even angrier.

"What an animal!" he exclaimed. "This is not a cow; it's a beast," he said, slamming the door shut. His wife, Mukarram was pouring water into the samovar to make some tea. "What an animal!" Boqayev said again. "We have to sell this cow and buy a pig instead."

"We cannot keep a pig; it is not allowed in the city," Mukarram said, as she was putting coal in the samovar. "Why? Are they not allowed? Who said so? Did I say that? Yes, that's right, of course, it's not allowed," Boqayev said.

"Come inside the house, Hamida came to visit," Mukarram told her husband. Hamida was a sixteen-year-old intelligent and cheerful girl. She was happy to see her sister's husband. "Oh, you're home! if I knew that, I would have brought my notebook with me. It's a pity I didn't bring it," she said.

Boqijon Boqayev's mood changed and he began to look happy; soon he forgot about the tick in the cow's ear and the pig ruining the barn's edges. "I heard that you transferred your studies from the institute to the college, is that true?" Boqijon asked. "Hmm . . . you did the right thing. Was I the one who told you to transfer? Hmm . . . I've been in anguish. The college of workers is a good college; I went there once. The word 'practicum' was written on the office door; that is not right. Practicum, minimum, maximum, all these words are Latin or are close to Latin. I personally think so."

They were quiet for a short while. "Boqijon," the girl said, feeling shy, "I wanted to ask you something. We read Chekov's "Desire to Sleep" in class, and we want to act it out. We want to judge the girl who killed the little child in the story. Rahima will play the role of the child's mother, Sharifjon will be the lawyer, and there will also be judges. As for me, I want to prove the girl innocent and blame her boss, who mercilessly took advantage of this girl. That's all I wrote for now. I wanted to know your opinion about this issue. Chekov wanted to say this, didn't he?"

Boqayev thought for a while and asked her, "Who teaches you the beautiful arts? Is it Hakimov? He is a stupid man; he does not improve himself. When I tell him that a question mark comes after 'what,' he laughs. But this is not the point."

Mukarram came in, holding a samovar. Hamida quickly got up from her place, took the samovar from her sister, and placed it on the table. She wanted to scold her sister's husband for not helping his pregnant wife, but she was shy and kept quiet. Boqijon Boqayev looked very thirsty, for he drank four cups of tea in a row and started to sweat.

"After eating *chuchvara*, drinking tea is very good," he said, wiping the sweat from his face. "Hmm . . . my beard has grown. If it weren't for barbers, people would have become monkeys. Monkeys have evolved into human beings. Engels has an opinion about this."

"Boqijon, you haven't told me your viewpoint about that subject," the girl said. "Isn't what I said Chekov's opinion also?" Boqijon asked for another cup of tea. "Chekov? Hmm . . . when talking about bourgeoisie realism, we have to look carefully at its objective before anything else. Objective realism should be understood just as bourgeoisie realists understand it and picture it. I suppose that Chekov's talents from the beginning until the end display primary bourgeoisie realism, which means . . . hmm . . . Mukarram, have you put an egg for the chickens? There must always be eggs in front of the chickens or else they will become wild. Dear God, there aren't more stupid creatures than chickens! They only lay eggs if there is an egg in front of them; why is that? And why does the rooster crow at dawn? It's a strange psychology, indeed. Are you studying biology?"

Hamida talked about what they had studied in biology and what they were going to study in the current year. She also mentioned that she wanted to use physiological reasons in the speech that she was going to say at the play and turned the discussion back to Chekov.

"Hmm . . ." began Boqayev again. "I have my own personal opinion about Chekov. As for others, let them say whatever they want. In my opinion, his point of view differs completely from that of Pushkin and Lermontov although all of these writers are from the same era, same social class, and same country."

"Chekov didn't live in the same era as Pushkin did. There's a picture of him and Maxim Gorky in our library; and Chekov probably died in 1904," Hamida replied.

Boqayev felt a little embarrassed. "Which Chekov are you talking about? Pour another cup of tea for me. About this Chekov? That's right, he died either in the first half of 1904 or in the second half of that year. Give me another handkerchief; this one smells like onions. As for me, I'm talking about that Chekov, the one who was a representative of the primary bourgeoisie realism."

"What about the story, "Desire to Sleep"? To which Chekov does it belong?" asked Hamida.

"To this Chekov, there's no doubt about that. This story was first published in 'Sovremennik' magazine."

After that, Boqijon Boqayev gave a long speech; however Hamida did not understand a single word of what he said. Boqijon talked about some kind of famous critic called Detirding who wrote to a writer called Shelling, "By the time you will be in need of a servant's help, your son will grow up and become a lad." He also said that Marx had classified Dobrolubov in the same list as Mering; and also that there was some kind of dramatist called Stending who, at his deathbed, wrote to the critic, Deming, "If God has created all creatures, I'm not amazed at them. Is a lizard even considered to be a creature?!" Hamida felt as if her head was very dizzy; she yawned twice without letting him notice.

It was already dark when Hamida said goodbye to the hosts of the house and went outside. Unfortunately, she did not get a single opinion about the story "Desire to Sleep" from her sister's husband. She kept wondering about what he had said to her, but there wasn't anything in her brain except for the words: practicum, minimum, maximum, Detirding, Stending, Shelling, Mering, Deming, . . .

The Brides' Revolution

by Said Ahmad

Usta Mahkam's youngest daughter, Inobat, grew up to be a very talkative girl. Her sisters and even her brothers' wives were very fearful of her. She said things that would affect any kind of person. Ever since she became a chatterbox, she never left any utterance without its response. Her strict aunt, whom Inobat resembled, said to her, "If your future mother-in-law turns out to be a humble, tolerant woman, you'll kill her. If a *hoji* mother can't deal with you, then any other woman will probably die."

Not only did Inobat annoy her brothers' wives, but she also annoyed all the others in the neighborhood. Inobat's mother refused two or three suitors' mothers, who came asking for Inobat, not because she didn't like them, but because she had mercy on them. The first suitor was a humble woman; Inobat would undoubtedly turn her into a dried apricot in two days. The other one was just like an angel; at the end of her every sentence, she added, "honey," "dear." If Inobat raised her voice at her, the woman would certainly faint.

And so, the mother who had refused several suitors, finally agreed to a mother who had asked Inobat's hand for her youngest son. Inobat's mother cut a loaf of bread from the loaves which the suitor had brought[5]. This woman, who lived five blocks away from Inobat's family, was called "the mother of the seven heroic brothers." She was known to everyone in the city, was strict with all her daughters-in-law, and was nick-named "the old general."

After the engagement, Inobat's aunt told her, "That's it; you're finished! Your mother-in-law will eat you alive."

"Eat me alive?! Whatever she'll try will be useless. I will make her go through the hole of a needle!" Inobat said, spitefully.

Anyway, she said this and the other said that and finally there was a wedding. Inobat became a very beautiful bride with just a little make-up. She blossomed like a flower the next day after her wedding. The wedding, of which numerous rumors were spread over the whole city, was finally over.

For three days, the six sisters-in-law washed the dishes, towels, and tablecloths. As for their mother-in-law, she sat under the terrace, saying her prayers, and not interfering with their work. Every once in a while, the middle daughter-in-law came to her to fix her pillow and renew her tea.

As for Inobat, she felt embarrassed just standing there not doing anything, so she helped her sisters-in-law. The middle daughter-in-law

---

5   According to Uzbek customs, matchmakers (suitors' mothers) come with eight or ten loaves of bread. The host of the house puts some of them on the table. If she agrees to the engagement, she cuts one of them into pieces, if not, she leaves them as they are.

prepared tea and went to her mother-in-law to sit with her under the terrace. Inobat's youngest sister-in-law, who was sitting next to her, gently poked her. "Do you see this spy? Be careful from her, for she is the old woman's agent." Inobat wondered and laughed to herself.

"Don't laugh, my dear sister-in-law. You'll know what I mean only when you experience it."

Not even a week had passed when all the secrets of this house had been revealed to Inobat. She was the seventh daughter-in-law in this house. The old woman had seven sons, whom she had raised and educated. Her sons never crossed their mother's line; they even brought their salaries and handed them to her every month. All seven sons and all seven daughters-in-law ate from one pot; not one of them could cook anything she willed by herself. The old woman kept the storeroom's key in her pocket all the time. Every day, she entered the kitchen with the required ingredients and did not leave until she saw the pot boiling. Whenever she left the house, the old woman trusted her middle daughter-in-law with these things. And even then, the key always stayed with her; she used to give the cooking ingredients in a paper bag to her daughter-in-law.

Of course the old woman never constrained her daughters-in-law's sustenance. But she acted according to a plan and she never liked to waste anything. During dinner, if there was any food left on the table, she babbled about it and forced everyone to eat it until it was all finished or if that did not work, she forced herself to eat it.

All her daughters-in-law worked as well. Every day after breakfast, the old woman went into her room and came out with her wallet. She gave each of her sons a *som*[6], each of her daughters-in-law half a som, and each of her grandchildren, who went to school, ten *tiyins*. Then, she went back in with her wallet.

On the fifteenth of every month, each of her sons and daughters-in-law handed in his/her salary to the old woman, one by one. Without hurrying, she counted the money and if the amount was less than a thousand soms, she frowned.

This old woman had another habit; at night when everybody went in to their rooms, she looked at the entrances of their rooms and examined their shoes. If she found shoes that needed any kind of mending, she collected them and the next day, she went to the shoe-maker and got them fixed by the end of the day.

In brief, this old woman was like a marshal. Everything, both big and small, was under her supervision. In the evenings, all seven families gathered under the woman's terrace to watch television together, since there was only one television in this house. If the old woman started yawning, the middle daughter-in-law immediately got up and turned off the TV, even if the show or movie they were watching was not over.

The daughters-in-law were all afraid of both the old woman and the middle daughter-in-law. If there was to be any argument in the house, this middle daughter-in-law was invariably the cause of it, for she would eavesdrop on her sisters-in-law's conversations during the night and the next day, she would tell the old woman

---

[6]   som: Uzbek currency; 100 tiyins make 1 som.

about what she had heard. Everything that was told during the night was announced the next morning, even before the sun rose.

In short, this house resembled a small kingdom, which had its own queen and minister, and which had its own rules and systems.

In the beginning, Inobat never paid attention to these things for she was still enjoying her life as a bride. For this reason, the middle daughter-in-law did not bother her, because she was still a new bride. But after a month had passed, Inobat's "faults" also started to be revealed.

One day, during breakfast, the old woman spilled the cup of tea on the yard which Inobat had poured and passed to her. "I don't drink tea which has been poured by a person whose heart is black," she said to Inobat. Inobat was astonished. The middle daughter-in-law poured another cup of tea, and bending a little forward, handed it to the old woman with her right hand, holding her right sleeve back with her left little finger. The old woman took it. Inobat also spilled her tea on the yard, got up from her place, went inside her room, and slammed the door shut. Her husband also wanted to get up and go to her, but one scowling look from the old woman made him stay in his place.

Inobat's youngest sister-in-law waited patiently until the old woman left to one of her cousin's house. She knocked on Inobat's window and the two started whispering to each other about something in a low voice so that the middle daughter-in-law, who was sweeping the terrace, would not hear anything.

"We have to teach the old woman a lesson; she has crossed her limit. We can't even talk about her to our husbands, because they get angry so easily." As soon as the middle daughter-in-law was done sweeping and left the house, carrying a basket, the six sisters-in-law assembled in front of the terrace and had a long discussion. When she got back, they separated and each went to her own room. Inobat was left by herself.

"Listen, you're a new person in this house. Don't listen to what these backbiters say to you. If you do as I tell you, everything will be alright. Do you know why mother spilled your tea which you handed to her?"

"No," replied Inobat, feeling interested to find out why.

"You passed the tea with your left hand; people who pass tea with their left hands have a black heart."

Inobat could not believe what she heard and said, "Oh and is that a reason? Did I get married to her or her son?! Tell her to just sit and pray for her children or else I'll make her go through a meat grinder!"

Her sister-in-law raised her eyebrows and said to her, "Oh God! You sure have a big mouth! When you listen to just two bitter words from mother, your sanity will return to you. But keep this in mind: in this house, the old woman is the decision-maker."

After this conversation, the old woman started treating Inobat without cordiality. However, the six sisters-in-law went on whispering and discussing something every day. What they were talking about was finally revealed one Sunday morning. When the old woman woke up and went to perform ablution, there was a red table cloth on the big table under the terrace. The sons and their wives all gathered, sat down, and silently waited for the old woman to finish praying. When she was done, Inobat called to her, "Come over here, mom!" The old woman seemed startled.

"What the hell is going on? Is this a house or an administration? And why have you all gathered? Is there a meeting going on?"

Inobat's sister-in-law said, "Not a meeting, it's a court trial! Come here, mother." The old woman mumbled something and started to walk away, when the eldest daughter-in-law called out, "If you don't come, then we'll declare the judgment by default." The old woman thought this a kind of joke, so she went to the terrace and sat down.

Inobat rose from her place and said, "The court is now in session. There is one case to be looked at: the complaints of seven daughters-in-law over their mother-in-law and to pronounce a verdict on the basis of criminal procedures. Does anyone have anything to add? No? Good, then let's proceed. Let's hear from the eldest daughter-in-law; plaintiff, you may now get up and speak."

The eldest daughter-in-law got up from her place, nervous. Not having the nerve to look at her mother-in-law in the face, she started talking, "It has been fourteen years since I came to this house as a bride. During these fourteen years, I felt as if I was living in a house for rent, and not in my own house. My husband is as limp as a rag. I've never felt comfortable in my marriage life. Maybe you don't believe me, but I swear I'm telling the truth. During the past years, I have *never*, by myself, cut a bunch of grapes from this garden yard. You can understand the rest yourselves."

She sat down and the next daughter-in-law stood up and said, "She always tells me, 'You are an actress's daughter. Your mother played the role of a witch on stage so don't sit in my place. Don't drink from my cup because you're going to cast a spell on me.' Seven years ago, I caught a cold and ever since then I've been called a 'snot.'"

The old woman tried to get up from her place and leave, but Inobat told her boldly, "Sit down!" Surprisingly, the old woman sat down and it was not clear whether she did this because of fear, bewilderment, or anger!

The middle daughter-in-law rose from her place and said, "I wish all mothers were like her for she is a role model. It's thanks to her that our sustenance is complete, and we are all happy from our heart. I haven't signed that complaint," implying that all that the others had said were lies.

The others immediately attacked her, "You're our mother-in-law's agent and you always tattletale to her about us. You only got closer to her after you helped her in getting her artificial teeth fixed. Who allowed you to talk anyway?"

The old woman got up from her place and shouted to her sons, "What kind of men are you? Your wives attack me and all you do is just watch?" Her sons dropped their heads, and laughed a concealed laugh, looking at the ground.

Inobat picked up her paper and said, "Listen. I announce the verdict. We all agree to live in this house on the condition that our mother-in-law gives us the storeroom's key, that she allows for every family to live an independent life, and that she does not take our salaries. If she does not accept our conditions, then we will leave the house. Our workplace will provide an apartment for each of us. So, do you agree?"

"Never!" the old woman exclaimed. She rose from her place, waved her hand, and went inside her room. Everyone stood in astonishment, with open mouths, and looked at each other, as if to say, 'What do we do now?' Inobat raised her voice, so as to make sure the old woman would hear her from her room, and said, "If our mother-in-law agrees to our conditions, then each one of us will give her five soms every month. Seven sons and seven sisters-in-law will give five soms each, which will be a total of seventy soms. Of course, the food and clothes will be at our expense."

The old woman, as if to say, 'Shut up!' slammed her door. The sisters-in-law lost hope in themselves after the useless trial and started looking at each other. Inobat winked at them and again said in a loud voice, "The decision is final! An hour will be given to either accept or reject the offer, and after an hour, each one of us will go to the market to bring a truck and will start moving to Chilonzor district. The court is adjourned. You may now leave."

The door slowly opened and the old woman's head popped out. "Even joking has its limits. Damn your actions!"

"This is no joke; this is serious and we expect you to give us your response within an hour."

The old woman slowly came back to her place, sat down, and said, "All right. What do you want me to do?"

"Give us our freedom," Inobat replied. "Your eldest daughter-in-law has three children so let her and the rest of us as well be responsible for our own livelihood by ourselves. You can choose whichever dish you like from the seven different kinds prepared by your seven daughters-in-law, with all respect."

"Are you saying that you want to cook in seven pots all in one day?"

"Of course, each one of us will eat what he/she desires."

The old woman muttered. "You have influenced your sisters-in-law who haven't said a word all these years and you have influenced my son as well," she said, looking at Inobat angrily.

"Do you agree or not?" asked Inobat, after the old woman had calmed a little.

The old woman got even angrier. "If you want to move out, then you can! I'll put the house for rent and I'll sue you and demand expenses."

Inobat hit the table with her palm and said, "Okay, there are five minutes left. One of you has to go to the market to bring a truck. We'll be moving in seven trucks."

The old woman got confused, and her eyes wandered, and she only spoke when the eldest daughter-in-law had reached the door. "Wait! Stop!" the old woman said and went inside her room. After awhile, she returned from her room, and threw the key at the yard. "Here, take it! If you want, you can cook in ten pots! How much could an old woman's stomach want anyway? Do as you wish!"

"We, together with your sons, have calculated the money that we have given you and the amount has reached sixteen thousand soms. So you have to distribute it among all of us."

"I won't give you anything! You won't have a single tiyin. Why do I have to give you the money that I have collected for my own funeral?"

All the sisters-in-law said at once, "Okay, okay, let her keep it. But from now on, she will not take anything." The old woman kept quiet, as if being thankful to have kept the money. That afternoon of the same day, the seven sons kindled a fire in seven places at the yard and during the evening, seven pots boiled at the same time.

The old woman's prestige and respect increased; her seven daughters-in-law were sweetly calling her from seven directions, "Mother, dinner is ready." "I've prepared dinner, mother. We're waiting for you." The old woman, still feeling angry, did not go to any one of them. As she was praying the asr prayer, the table under the terrace was filled with different kinds of foods: soup, osh, laghmon, shovla, chuchvara, and qovurma. The old woman ate a few spoonfuls of each one and said to herself, "My little one is quite a cook." The old woman was showered with respect. One of her daughters-in-law had set the table, the other made her some tea, a third cleaned her shoes, a fourth gave her a perfumed soap, and the youngest daughter-in-law brought her a big glass of watermelon juice. As if all this wasn't enough, she wrapped her mother-in-law's shoulders with a shawl and said, "If you wear this at night, you will not catch a cold, my dear mother."

The old woman was still not satisfied. But when she lied down and closed her eyes, she finally admitted that what her daughters-in-law had done was just. "I was giving myself a hard time all this time. Is this all necessary to me?! Let them do what they want. Who told me to become a *hoji* mother in the first place?" She went to sleep with these thoughts in her mind. Ever since she started getting her sons married, this was the first time that she slept without worries in her mind.

The eldest daughter-in-law turned off the lamp, thinking that it might wake up her mother-in-law. As for the middle daughter-in-law, she could not get used to this new habit so she kept on walking in the yard at night, listening to her sisters-in-law's conversations under the windows. The next morning, she was about to whisper something into the old woman's ear, when she interrupted her and said, "My daughter, stop your habit. I quit from my job of being the *hoji* mother and I also free you from being a spy." All her daughters-in-law heard this and started laughing out loud. And for the first time in fifteen years, seven samovars boiled at the same time in this house.

The Bride from the City

By Nargiza Ghulomova

The dawn wipes away the last traces of the night from the sky, but the sun still has not risen. High mountains are blocking it. Dogs are barking; roosters are crowing. The village is starting to wake up. Daughters-in-law, carrying buckets and brooms, appear in yards. If one were to sacrifice his/ her sleep and go outside, he/ she would witness a most wonderful scene. All daughters-in-law are wearing dazzling dresses that attract the eyes; thousands of kinds of *atlas*[7] can be seen. It is as if they have come out for a dress exhibition, and not to sweep their front yards. After all the cleaning is done, flowers and trees blossom and bloom. The sun starts to peep from behind the mountains. Houses in which there are no daughters-in-law are going to be opened a little late today. Mothers whose daughters have reached the age of marriage try to protect their daughters and let them get enough hours of sleep. When the sun has completely risen, the door of the house at the far end of the street opens and Rano appears, carrying a bucket. She is wearing a faded cotton dress and on her head is a yellow scarf covering her forehead down to her eyebrows. Rano lazily sprinkles the water from her bucket onto the yard and goes back inside. She lies down on the bed, next to her snoring husband. Her footsteps have awoken her mother-in-law, Jannat. "There, she has sprinkled the water. Now, did she go to the kitchen? No." Jannat gets up from her bed, scowling. She prepares

---

[7] atlas: national Uzbek dress

breakfast, making lots of loud noises. Qudrat senses his wife's mood from the way she holds the teapot.

"Where are the others?" Qudrat bites his lips as soon as he asks. He wishes he hadn't asked that question.

"Where else would they be in the early morning? They must still be sleeping and having sweet dreams! Others' yards are constantly glowing; as for ours, the broom barely touches it. Two years have passed and she still hasn't gotten used to it! Worse, she has become a sleeper as well. I told you before several times that a city bride is not appropriate for us at all," Jannat replies with all her voice, as if speaking to the neighbors and not her husband.

"Maybe . . ." says her husband in a low voice.

"Maybe? She has yet to give us grandchildren. There is no hope in your daughter-in-law. If there happens to be a wind, she bends before the basil does!"

Qudrat gives his wife a peculiar look. "Did you forget that you also didn't get pregnant for five years?" he asks.

"That's exactly my point. Since he is my one and only son, I want him to have as many children as possible. Those from the city give birth to only one or two," replies his wife.

"This is not a city. May God give us many grandchildren that you may not even have enough time to do anything else but to look after them!" Qudrat exclaims.

Jannat starts crying. "Your daughter-in-law does not respect me. Other daughters-in-law call their mothers-in-law "mother." But she . . ." Jannat could not complete her sentence.

"Dear, if she called you mother, will something be added to your name Jannat? Our daughter-in-law is very polite and well-behaved. In the past two years, she never misbehaved. Those daughters-in-law who call their mothers-in-law mother, you cannot imagine how much trouble they cause them."

"Can't a person have hopes and dreams?" Jannat asks.

"Your son and Rano have a very romantic relationship; just look at them treating each other as if they are love birds. This means that you have achieved your hopes and dreams, so be grateful!" her husband replies.

As soon as their son, Umid, comes in, Qudrat changes his expression. "Good morning, son. Did you sleep okay?" he asks.

Jannat starts again, "Where is your beloved wife? Is she still sleeping? What does she do all night anyway?"

"That's enough!" says Qudrat in a serious tone. Umid does not say anything. He had already understood that it was useless to discuss this issue with his mother. Soon, Rano appears and greets everyone. Feeling embarrassed and not knowing what to say or do, she keeps looking at the floor. Her mother-in-law does not respond to her greeting and turns her head away. Her father-in-law wants to rescue her from this awkward situation, so he says, "Come and sit down. Your tea will get cold." It was so quiet during breakfast that a pin drop could have been heard. After breakfast, all family members say their prayers, get up, and leave to do their work. Only Rano is left. She clears up the breakfast table and washes the dishes. Then, she goes to her room and lies down on the couch. She is deep in her thoughts; she has lived with this family for two years now but everything still seems temporary to her. Is it possible that she will spend her entire life here, where tall mountains are always surrounding her from all directions, where the scorching sun seems to rise almost from midnight, and where the village's cows and donkeys pass from here and there, dusting everywhere? All this seems like a dream to Rano. It is as if she would wake up any minute and return to her own hometown, to the embrace of her own parents. If she had not loved her husband, she would have left a long time ago. But she fell in love with Umid when she first met him at her friend's wedding. It was love at first sight for her. In the beginning, Rano's mother was against them getting married, but Rano was very stubborn. As for her father, he was also on her side. Her father also liked the serious, independent Umid.

After their wedding, Umid's love for Rano took control over her and everything around her seemed beautiful in her eyes. But as time passed, nature's beauty, the pure air of the mountains, and even her husband's love turned into casual everyday things. Everything started to seem boring to Rano. To top it all off, her mother-in-law's wanting Rano to call her 'mother' was too much.

*   *   *

Rano missed her own mother very much. While she was looking sadly at the road that would take her to the city, her husband came from behind her and wrapped his arms around her shoulders. "Do you miss your home?" he asked her.

"Yes," she responded.

"Rano, can I ask a favor of you?" he asked again. Rano looked at her husband with a questioning look. "Call my mom 'mother'," he said.

Rano sighed deeply. She said, "You know, my mother is my best friend and advisor. I tell her all my secrets. She is a very amazing woman. And yet, until this day, I've never called her 'mother,' not even once."* Umid did not say anything, but after this, he did not seem interested in his wife's needs. He left immediately to work.

Even though Rano never talked to her mother-in-law in a rude way and she did all her house chores perfectly, their relationship worsened. One day, while she was in the midst of her day-dreams, she felt a weird taste in her mouth. She got up and ran outside to the back yard. She went over to one corner and squatted down. Her mother-in-law, who was standing a few meters away busy with her work, looked at Rano and observed her.

In the evening, while Rano was sweeping the front yard outside her house, the neighbor's son, Rustam, came running towards her. "Rano, are you feeling well today? I was watching you from the roof when you ran out to the yard; your face was completely pale!" he exclaimed.

"Oh, everything's okay. I guess it's something I ate," Rano replied.

Although Rustam is a thirteen or fourteen-year-old boy, he looked much younger than that, because God had made him short for his age. Despite this, he was respected by all the other village boys. He could not understand his relationship to Rano, but he knew that he had become very attached to her and he greatly respected her. He could not stand Umid, however. Rano liked this sweet boy's kindness. It could be said that Rustam was her only friend in the entire village. There were times when he would be the only person to support her.

"Allow me to do the sweeping for you," Rustam offered.

"No, what will people say?" Rano said.

"Let them say whatever they want. I just don't want you to get ill. And besides, you're very thin," he said.

"That's very thoughtful of you, Rustam," Rano said, smiling.

"It's nothing. Just take care of yourself. Where's your crazy husband, by the way? Can't he help you even a little bit?" Rustam asked.

"Don't say that. He has a lot of work to do," Rano replied.

"I don't agree. Last year's snow is more useful than him," Rustam said and ran to where the other boys were playing football.

That night, Rano could not sleep at all. When she was finally starting to drift off, her husband poked her and said, "Wake up, it's morning." Rano gave her husband an unpleasant look but got up from bed. As soon as she went out to the front yard outside her house, she smiled. The yard was perfectly swept and sprinkled with water. "This is Rustam's work," Rano understood quickly. She went inside, swept the garden yard, and sprinkled water. Although she wanted to go back to sleep, she entered the kitchen and started preparing breakfast.

As usual, everybody assembled round the breakfast table and started having breakfast. Rano glanced at her mother-in-law from the corner of her eye. No traces of change at all; Rano lost hope. What's the point of preparing breakfast then? The minute she lifted a piece of bread to her mouth, she again felt the same weird taste in her mouth. She immediately got up and hurriedly went out. "It seems as if Rano is not feeling well," Qudrat said to Jannat. "I think you better take her to the doctor."

"Nothing has happened to her," his wife replied coldly. "This is how she is!" Umid suddenly stopped eating, said his prayers, and hurriedly went out after his wife.

Qudrat said to his wife, "You have waited for this for a long time. I'm not even sensing your happiness. Look, Rano has really tried hard today! Can't you just cheer up a little?"

"The neighbors are laughing at me," Jannat started crying again. "They're saying, 'your daughter-in-law doesn't respect you. If you couldn't get her to say mother in two years, then you won't be able to control her after this.'"

Her husband could barely hold his laughter. "You don't have to let the whole village know what's going on. If even a small thing happens in our house, it's heard loud and clear at the neighbor's. If this means so much to you, then just speak to Rano directly."

"I did speak to her, but she is very stubborn. Maybe she'll listen to you," Jannat said, looking at her husband with pleading eyes.

"I cannot . . ." Qudrat did not know what else to say. "All right, all right, I'll try."

Rano was ironing her husband's shirt in the terrace. Seeing her father-in-law approaching her, she got up from her place. "My daughter," he started, "don't be upset about your mother-in-law. She's actually a very kind woman. She likes you. Believe me, when you'll have children, she'll spoil them with attention and love." Rano did not say anything. Noticing that her eyes were red, Qudrat sensed that she had been crying. "Maybe you miss your mother?" he asked. This time, Rano nodded her head. "I'll tell Umid to take you to the city. You'll stay at your parents' house for a couple of days."

Father and son leaft to work. Jannat also got dressed and went out somewhere. Rano was left all by herself. "Rano," called Rustam from above the roof. He jumped down, got several peaches from his sleeve, and gave them to her. "Here, these are for you," he said.

"Thanks," she replied.

"From now on, I'll bring you fruits every day. You have to start eating properly now," he said.

"Why are you saying that?" Rano asked.

"Because you're gonna be a mom soon," Rustam answered.

"Where did you get this from? Who told you this?" Rano asked, confused.

"The whole village knows this. Everybody's talking about it," Rustam replied casually.

"I myself am not aware of this. How come they know?" Rano asked.

"Yesterday your mother-in-law came to our house and told us. You should've seen how happy she was, she even started crying!" Rustam said excitedly.

"No way!" Rano could not believe what she was hearing.

"If I'm lying, let the heavens take my soul!" exclaimed Rustam. "Starting from now, you have to take good care of yourself."

"So that's why you had swept the yard for me today?" asked Rano, smiling.

"I didn't do it," Rustam said.

"Why are you lying? Then who else?" Rano asked.

"It could be angels," Rustam innocently replied.

Rano started laughing. "Of course, if that makes you an angel. Don't do it again; I can handle it myself. But thanks anyway."

"You're welcome. But you know, you get up very late. You're the last person to come out," Rustam told her.

"So what? The sprinkled water on others' front yards will dry up until the sun rises whereas mine will stay fresh and damp."

Rustam burst into laughter. "You're a strange person, Rano," he said. "That's not what I meant. Early in the morning, even before the sun rises, angels fly above houses. Those angels leave blessings in houses whose yards are cleaned and swept and whose doors are opened. Rano, could I ask you something?"

"Of course," Rano replied.

"How come you do not have any friends here in the village? Or are you different from the others?" he asked.

"Of course, I'm different. Otherwise, I would not leave the city and come to this village, where God's mercy doesn't seem to reach."

"Don't you like it here?" Rustam asked sadly.

"No," answered Rano.

"Then are you gonna leave?" he asked again.

"Yes, I am, but don't be sad. Whenever I'll pass by here, I'll definitely give you a visit. That's of course, as long as you also don't leave here."

"I will *never* leave here!" proudly exclaimed Rustam.

That evening, Rano prepared dinner and as soon as she finished, she ran outside to the yard. She almost caught her breath when she saw the sun setting behind the mountains. It seemed as if everywhere was glittering like gold under the effect of the sun's last rays. "How wonderful!" Rano said to herself. "I can't believe I didn't notice until this moment." She again felt a strange taste in her mouth. However, it quickly went away and Rano was in a very good mood. She slowly placed her hands on her tummy and again spoke to herself, "Is it possible that I'm really going to be a mom?" Suddenly, her sweet thoughts were interrupted by her father-in-law calling her to dinner.

The evening was very beautiful, with stars covering the whole sky. The new moon peeped through the open bedroom window and woke up Rano. The night had a special kind of magical silence that not even the echo of an owl's howling from the mountains could break. Rano got up from bed; she was wearing a new, warm robe that her mother had given her as a present and on her head was a golden decorated scarf. Rano sat down at the top of the stairs and looked towards the dark mountains. They looked very magnificent under the moonlight. "These mountains will protect my child and me from any kind of bad omens," Rano said to herself. At this moment, she herself was astonished at the way she was thinking. "What's happening to me?" she asked herself.

Finally, it was time for dawn to replace night. The moon and the stars slowly started to fade away. Rano was still sitting and staring at the mountains opposite her. After a few moments, the sun will rise from behind these mountains and spread its warm rays to the world. Rano felt happy at the thought of this. Finally, traces of morning began to appear. A new day was beginning. Rano felt as if she was a part of this magical morning and at this moment, she at last found the answer to her question: just like this beginning day, motherly feelings were beginning in her. Rano got up and went down the stairs; her steps were very light. She swept the front yard and garden and sprinkled water. Then, she went into the kitchen and prepared breakfast. After a little while, Jannat entered the kitchen. "Good morning, mother!" Rano's voice shook for she had uttered the word 'mother' unwillingly.

Jannat's face glowed and her eyes sparkled, but she did not reply right away. "Good morning, my daughter. Did you sleep well?" she finally said.

"I slept very well, mother. Today, I greeted dawn."

"Did you like it?" asked her mother-in-law.

"Of course I liked it. I didn't know it would be this beautiful." Soon, father and son entered the kitchen. Jannat's warm relationship with Rano gave the breakfast a special flavor and the conversation got interesting.

When Umid and Rano were left alone, he said, "Rano, it's been a long time since we have gone out together. Why don't we go to the city today and have some fun?"

"I wonder what mother will say," Rano said in a soft and quiet voice. She actually began to like the way she talked.

"You can go, my children, you can go," said Jannat, who heard them talking. "Just make sure to be here by dinner time. The food will not taste as good as when you are here," she added. As soon as the couple left, Jannat took a dish in her hand and also headed towards the door.

"Where are *you* going?" asked her husband in a loud voice.

"I want to go to one of our neighbor's and bring some cream. Our daughter-in-law likes *chuchvara* very much," Jannat replied.

"So what does cream have to do with this?" Qudrat asked.

"It's because Rano doesn't eat *chuchvara* except with cream," Jannat replied, smiling.

* Some comments on this story:

Firstly, this is a social story that displays one of the most difficult circumstances in the life of Uzbek society, which is the relationship between the mother-in-law and daughter-in-law. The majority of Uzbek girls, after getting married, live in their husbands' houses with his parents. It is the daughter-in-law's responsibility to serve the family, which includes sweeping the front yard and also the yard inside, as we have read in this story.

Secondly, in Uzbek society, daughters-in-law call their mothers-in-law 'mother' and fathers-in-law 'father' and by saying this, they show respect towards their parents-in-law. Also, sons-in-law call their parents-in-law mother and father or mom and dad. This is considered very normal and accepted in Uzbek society. There is also another way of addressing while talking, which is by adding 'jon' to the name of the person or to 'mother' and 'father.' 'Jon' signifies additional respect, love, and care. We could say that 'jon' is the equivalent of 'dear' in English. Hence in the Uzbek language, 'dear mother' would be 'oyijon' and 'dear father' would be 'dadajon,' respectively.

In the above story, the reason why Jannat asks Rano to call Jannat 'mother' is to show others that her daughter-in-law respects her.

The Grandfather and his Grandson

By Toghay Murod

A three-year-old grandson gets up from his bed before everyone else. He enters the living room, wearing red shoes, green pants, and a shirt. The people who are sitting around the table do not pay attention to him, and he keeps standing in the corridor for a while.

Whoever looks at the child from the front noticing his big ears just as if they were placed there temporarily, will think that he looks like his uncle. And whoever looks at his black eyes, fat nose, wide forehead, and rosy cheeks that never knew what distress was, will think that he looks like his father.

The grandson gets down the stairs quietly and looks back. Then, with little steps, he heads towards the motorcycle standing near the door of the yard. He stands beside it and remembers that he rode on this beautiful seat with his father. This motorcycle had made loud noises and had moved fast; afraid, he had hugged his father and had closed his eyes. And now here he is, wanting to ride this motorcycle again. He holds the backseat, almost as if to demonstrate his desire to ride it.

After a while, his father comes and asks, "Where are you going?"

"I want to go with you," the son replies.

"Go where?" asks his father again.

"To work," the son answers.

"Yeah, yesterday our boss asked about you in a teacher's meeting and said, 'Why didn't he come to work?'" said his father, joking. The grandson does not understand what his father tells him. He is even hearing some of the words for the first time. But he understands that there is someone, either his aunt or uncle's wife, who says, "Let him come." And indeed, he will go, God willing, he will go. At that moment, his father presses something and the motorcycle produces a sound. The grandson shivers and moves his eyelashes swiftly.

He frowns, as if to say, "If you'll not take me with you, I'll cry." His father does not pay attention to him and leaves. The grandson stays where the motorcycle has left smoke. Now he wants to lie down on the ground and cry, but his grandfather, he is strict, and does not let his grandson lie down on the soil and cry until he feels okay. He takes his grandson's hand and leads him inside. Among the people that the grandson knows, he likes his grandfather the most, although he is strict. From now on, he will like his grandfather even more, because now the grandfather takes some chocolates from the cupboard and gives them to his grandson.

The grandson wants something. A few days ago, he went out with his grandfather; there, he saw high buildings and many people sitting in the streets, selling apples and cucumbers. At that time, his grandfather had bought him delicious water. Even now the grandson remembers that moment and wets his lips. Now he wants to tell his grandfather to take him there again but he cannot because he does not know where the place is.

He sits on his grandfather's lap and pesters him. His grandfather tells him, "Calm down, look there. Now look there, look at the children." He points to the television, which is placed in the corner.

The grandson had known for a little while that this big box which is half made from glass was called 'television'; but until now he is not able to pronounce its name. Suddenly, the grandfather laughs while watching something interesting in the television. His grandson joins him and laughs with him, although he does not understand what's going on. He just watches the show and wonders to himself, "How can so many people fit in such a small box?"

"Hey grandpa, where are those people?" asks the grandson.

"Inside the television, my boy," answers his grandfather.

"Are there houses inside?" asks the grandson again.

"Yes, my boy, yes, there's everything inside," replies the grandfather.

"Do they have chocolate too?" asks the grandson. The young grandson thinks that the best and most important thing to people in the world is chocolate. That is why he compares every single thing to chocolate. The grandson's question is left unanswered. The grandfather turns off the TV after the show is over and goes outside. The grandson sits leaning on the wall. He looks at the TV for awhile.

He puts his finger in his mouth and moves his head a little to the left. Then he comes closer to the TV and listens—nothing. He doesn't see those people anymore; just a while ago they were inside the TV . . . where did they go?

He wonders and looks inside the house. He sees his little toy car near the heater and comes closer to it. He pulls his sister's bride doll from its leg and lets it sit on his car. Then he pulls his car with a long string tied to it and goes outside. He looks at his grandfather who is working on something in the corner. He is making a window frame for a window. In front of him are all the needed tools and woods of different sizes. With a small pencil, he measures the wood and marks on it, and then he places the pencil behind his ear. His grandson watches him and laughs, and looks for a pencil to do the same, but does not find any. He pulls his car and heads towards the middle of the trees.

His grandfather keeps an eye on his grandson as he goes on with work. It has been almost two months since the grandfather's retirement, and the government had honored him. Before retiring, he used to think, "When will I retire and rest?" His wish of retirement did come true but now he cannot find a place to put himself and does not know what to do. And the one who goes back to work cannot always lie down and rest. The grandfather takes care of the yard, fixes anything that needs to be fixed—walls that have broken cracks, broken doors and windows,—and also takes care of the grape trees' branches. He does not rest until he fixes every single thing that needs fixing in the yard. "This is Ismail . . . Oh God, I repent to you. I have worked in the government for forty years and had to deal with thousands of people, but I cannot even live with this little kid for two months!"

Today is the second day that the grandfather is building a door for the chicken house. He measures the wood with his hand, gets confused, and measures it one more time. Only this time he marks it with a pencil. After that, he picks up a saw to cut it.

"It is not useful that I retired; for when I worked, at least ten people a day used to ask about me, but now no one even cares about me." The grandfather thinks about a lot of things, and remembers that his grandson had gone to play among the trees and glances at him to check on him. As he continues with his work, the grandfather feels sorry for his grandson. "It's hard for him, for there are no children to play with. Since everyone here leaves both of us together, do they mean to say, 'Both of you play together,' . . . No, it can't be."

The grandson, who is a little chubby, gets bored from playing, so he pulls his car along with him. He looks at the chicken house and notices a chicken that is hatching an egg. He kicks the soil with his left leg to chase the chicken away but it does not move from its place. The grandson thinks to himself, "All the chickens are playing in the yard, so then why is this chicken sitting all by itself?" He wants to break the bride doll's hand to throw it at the chicken, but realizes that he cannot break it. He picks up a small stone from the ground and throws it at the chicken. The chicken crows and leaves its nest, running away. The grandson sees an egg in the chicken's nest. He stretches his hand but his hand does not reach. So he enters the chicken house, crawling on his hands and legs. He takes the egg, puts it on his car, and goes to his grandfather. He tells him,

"Grandpa, the chicken's laid an egg, here it is!" "That's good," his grandfather replies. "Its egg is so warm," the grandson says.

Holding each other's hands, the grandfather and his grandson walk under the grapevines. The little grandson looks at some grapes hanging from the grapevines. He wants to pull them by himself and eat them, so he stretches his hand to the grapes just like his grandfather does, but the grapes are far, far away.

The grandfather looks at his grandson, and suddenly remembers his own childhood, and he feels as if something arises in his heart, something towards his grandson, and he keeps looking at his grandson's wide forehead and calm face.

The Rainbow

By Normurod Norqobulov

"Do you want to run away again?" A sweet little boy with dark black eyes, who had been peeping outside from a hole in the high wooden fence, was startled. Blinking his eyes, he turned to where the voice came from. Raising her eyebrows, his kindergarten teacher stood under the apricot tree and looked at him. "Don't even think about running away! Or else I will pull your ears," his teacher threatened. "Go and play with your friends." The little boy frowned; reluctantly, he went to the playground, where other little children were happily playing. One little girl hid her doll behind her back, thinking that he would take it away from her. But the little boy did not even pay attention to her. He picked up a broken toy car under his feet and started playing with it. However, he quickly got bored, so he threw it away and started running around in the playground.

Kindergarten was extremely boring to the little boy. Although it had been more than a week since he had started kindergarten, he still had not gotten used to it. He missed the sweet moments that he spent with his grandmother. When he was with her, he never got bored.

*   *   *

The little lamb in the barn was his closest friend. As usual after having breakfast, his grandmother would sit on a bench under the grapevines and would start to sew. As for the little boy, he would trod off to the barn and pester the little lamb, who would be quietly sitting in a corner. "Where's your mother?" he would ask him. The little lamb, as if understanding him, would say, "Maaa" in a soft, sweet voice. The little boy, pretending to understand, would say in a regretful voice, "Oh, she left to the farm?" The little lamb would again plead, "Maaa" in a pleading manner. "Don't cry," responded the little boy, imitating his grandmother. "You're a big boy now; it would be a shame for you to cry!" He started caressing the little lamb. The lamb liked this and smelled the little boy's hand and face. The boy searched the lamb's head and found its horns. "Hey, your horns are coming out!" he said, amazed. Then he searched his own head and said, "I don't have any, but I will soon, and when I do, we'll wrestle like this." He banged his forehead on the lamb's head as if to wrestle with him, but the poor lamb got frightened and moved back. However, the little boy did not leave him alone. The lamb made pleading noises, almost as if to ask the boy to stop.

The little boy heard his grandmother's voice coming from the yard, "Nurbek, don't torture the lamb!"

The little boy was genuinely sad from this. "Cry baby!" he said. "Go away! I'll never play with you again." He went out of the barn and observed the white and yellow chicks running around in the yard. Although he wanted to play with them, he was afraid of the mother hen who seemed to watch her chicks closely. The little boy walked towards the garden that was separated from the yard by a wired net. To this little boy, this garden was not just simply a garden; rather it was a world of wonders. There was a great deal of things in the garden that would amaze him. For instance, today, he saw a pink flower that had bloomed as big as a palm. He carefully held the flower from its stem and smelled it, just like the way his mother did. But he noticed that the flower already had an owner; a frightened bee flew away when the little boy touched the flower. He had heard from his grandmother that bees drink the flowers' nectar. He also wanted to drink so he examined the flower. Not finding anything, he sadly said, "It's drank all of it!" He went to examine another flower but as soon as he moved a few steps, he came across a totally different thing. The trees' trunks were painted white. It seemed to him as if they were wearing white pants. He got excited and yelled to his grandmother, "Grandma, hey grandma! Who did this to the trees?"

"What? What do you say, my dear?" replied his grandmother, without lifting her head.

Standing from behind the wired net, the little boy pointed to the trees and asked again, "Who did this to the trees?"

"Your mother," replied his grandmother without paying attention.

"Why?" asked the little boy, curiously.

"To keep away the insects," answered the grandmother.

"What will happen if insects crawl on trees?" asked the inquisitive, little boy.

"Something bad will happen," responded his grandmother. The little boy had heard this sentence from his grandmother lots of times. Whenever he did something wrong, his grandmother always said,

"Don't do that, my dear, or something bad will happen." In the little boy's mind, whenever his grandmother said this, something dreadful was implied. However, this time, he wondered deeply. Just yesterday, when he wanted to push a stick inside an ant house, his grandmother had said the same thing and had explained how ants are innocent, harmless creatures. However, today . . .

He asked his grandmother again, "Grandma, why will something bad happen?"

"What?" said his grandmother.

"What will happen if insects crawl on trees?" repeated the little boy.

His grandmother sensed that she could not get away with this question easily. She tried to find an appropriate answer. "What will happen if insects crawl? . . . The tree's trunk will itch and it won't produce any fruits," she finally said. Imagining the insects crawling on his own body, the little boy shivered. He went over to an apple tree and witnessed a shocking scene: although the trunk was thickly painted in white, several insects were crawling all over a big apple. The little boy picked up a stick to sweep away the ants from the apple. However, for some reason, he couldn't bring himself to do it. So he just stood there, hesitating.

At this same moment, his grandmother appeared in the garden. She collected a bunch of wild plants and handed it to her grandson, saying, "Take these and give them to your lamb." The little boy plopped the plants in front of the lamb and watched with great enthusiasm, as the lamb ate. Soon, he also wanted to taste the grass. He put a piece of grass in his mouth, chewed it, and not liking it, spat it out. He wiped his mouth on his sleeve and returned to the garden.

He spotted his dog tied to an apricot tree. He felt a great desire to play with him. He went near the dog to untie the rope but realized he was too weak to do it. He then went to his grandmother and begged her, "Grandma, please release my dog."

"If I release him, he'll eat all of the chicks," replied his grandmother.

"He won't touch them, he promised!" said the little boy, with confidence.

His grandmother smiled and said, "So you even talked with him?"

"Yes!" he said, grinning.

"Let's wait until your father returns from work," said his grandmother. "I'm also not strong enough to untie the rope."

The little boy believed her. He squatted down near his grandmother to help her pull out the unneeded weeds. However, since he was a little kid, he could not tell the difference between carrots and wild grass, so he pulled out both of them. His grandmother told him to go and play, so once again he headed off to the garden.

*   *   *

All of a sudden, his grandmother passed away and the little boy's entertaining, cheerful world turned upside down. His parents left to work early and returned home late, so they registered him in a newly built kindergarten in the village. He started getting bored from the very first day he went to the kindergarten. The next day, he cried and refused to go. Two days later, of course he did not even think of going there. But everything happened unexpectedly.

That same day, after lunch, when the little boy was playing around in the playground, he discovered an unfamiliar world from the hole in the wooden fence: between two prairies was a blue canal of flowing stream. The prairies stretched far into the hills. Herds of sheep were grazing on the grass. He also noticed a wooden bridge in the direction opposite of him and under that bridge, tanned boys were swimming. Farther away from these boys, the little boy observed a tall, thin boy in his early teens sitting by himself with a fishing rod.

The little boy had never left the village before. His caring grandmother had made sure that he was always near her. He was so fascinated at this unfamiliar and magical world that he did not even realize that he had crawled from under the wooden fence and got out of the kindergarten. After getting up, looking here and there, he felt as if he were lost. He went near the boy who was fishing. Near the boy, he saw a bucket full of moving fish. "Wow!" he cried, amazed.

The tall boy put his finger on his lips and said, "Hush! You'll scare away the fish!"

The little boy did not even pay attention to him. "Please give me one," he pleaded, without taking his eyes off the bucket.

The boy inspected the little kid from head to foot and asked, "What will you do with it?"

"I'll play with it," the little kid answered innocently.

"Play with it?" asked the boy, laughing. "What? Is a fish a toy to you?"

"Please give it to me, I really wanna play," the little kid begged.

At this moment, the hook of the fishing rod started moving, churning up the water. The boy hurriedly pulled the fishing line. A fish the size of a thumb glowed in the sun and landed on the grass. It started jumping up and down. The boy released it from the hook and threw it in the bucket. "Please give me this one," pleaded the little kid again.

"What an annoying brat you are! Go to your kindergarten!" the boy said.

"You're so greedy!" said the little boy, feeling sad. But the tall boy did not pay attention to him at all. He placed all of his concentration on the hook. The little boy stood there for awhile. Then he took a long stick lying on the floor and dipped its end in the water.

"What are you doing?" asked the tall boy, bewildered. Since the little boy was still sad from him, he did not answer. "So you think this is the way to fish? Without a hook?" the boy smiled. "Come over here and hold this well," he gave his fishing rod to the little boy. The little boy gladly took the rod and stared at the hook. He felt as if he had grown up. He looked at the tall boy appreciatively.

After some time, the hook started moving very quickly. The little boy did not know what to do. "Pull, pull! C'mon!" the rod's owner cried. The little boy got very confused. When the boy reached out to the rod, the little boy pulled. Unfortunately, he was too late; the fish had already eaten the worm and gotten away. "What kind of a fisher are you?" the boy muttered, placing another worm on the hook. "You let the fish get away."

The little boy, as if he had done something wrong, felt guilty and his head drooped. The tall boy eventually calmed down after mumbling for awhile. He took one fish from the bucket and gave it to the little boy. "Here, you can play with this. Now, go away from here." The little boy happily took the fish. Without taking his eyes off of it, he walked towards the boys who were swimming. The fish, which had been moving in his palm, completely stopped when the little boy reached the boys. When he was looking at the fish, puzzled, one by one, the boys started crowding up.

"Is that a fish?" one of them asked.

"How small!" another exclaimed.

"Oh no, it's dead!" another added.

"Did Rustam, the greedy, really give you this fish? Wow!"

"Throw it in the water, it'll come back to life."

"No, it won't."

"Yes, it will."

"Hey, let me see."

The little boy felt confused and lost in the midst of the boys' noises. The fish went from hand to hand until someone finally threw it in the canal. In an instant, all the boys spread out. As for the little boy, he ran happily, saying, "The fish came back to life!"

That day, he returned home at sunset, covered with dirt from head to foot. His mother had been very worried. She was waiting very nervously for her child. As soon as she saw him, she kissed and hugged him. Then she started scolding him and asking him where he had been all day. But he stood silent, lowering his head, because he was still under the effects of the events of his day at the canal. After he had eaten his dinner, he mumbled a few rambling things about the fisher boy and the fish that came back to life in the canal, and feeling extremely tired, he fell fast asleep.

The next day, the little boy was playing in the playground at his kindergarten. Black clouds covered the sky and it started raining. The screaming little children gathered under the terrace, seeking shelter from the rain. "Oh dear, we're in the beginning of summer, so why is it raining?" said the cook of the kindergarten, while covering her pot with the lid.

"Look, it's raining very heavily on the hills," said the kindergarten teacher, pointing to the hills.

"It'll stop in awhile," said another.

Indeed, the black clouds that had come from the east poured all their water over the hills and dissipated. Soon, the sun was shining and the smell of the damp grass was floating in the air. The cook tasted the food in her pot and made some tea. A short while later, all the women gathered to drink tea and have a chat. The little boy again remembered his grandmother; he sighed deeply and went over to the playground. He took advantage of his teachers being busy talking and crawled from under the fence and got outside. Nobody was there at the canal, but the little boy did not care. Glancing here and there, he walked towards the bridge. Life continued around him. The canal that was clear and pure yesterday became dirty and muddy today. A little far away, two sheep were wrestling with all their power with each other. Above in the sky, almost touching the clouds, falcons were flying. A man was speeding on a horse towards the farm. Three boys were racing each other on their bicycles on the road. An old man and his donkey were coming from the opposite direction. The boys frightened the donkey as they whizzed by. The old man, muttering something, waved his stick at them. The little boy stood observing the things going on around him. When the clouds that were temporarily covering the sun completely moved away, the little boy stared in amazement. He sighed and whispered to himself, "Aaah, what was that called?" Above the hills was a beautifully glittering rainbow with all its bright colors: red, blue, orange, green, yellow, and violet. The little boy was awestruck by the rainbow's various colors. Without even realizing, he started running towards the rainbow. But at that moment . . .

"Nurbek!" He quickly turned around and saw his kindergarten teacher pacing hurriedly towards him. "Nurbek, come back here!" The little boy just stood there, between his teacher and the rainbow, torn.

Aaah, how he wished his teacher would turn into his grandmother and take him to the rainbow . . .

Ramazon

by Oydin Hojiyeva

No matter who asks "What's your name?" from my sister's son, Ramazon, he answers, "Ramazon Mulla."

As soon as it is evening, my mother starts worrying and thinking, "What will Ramazon do this evening?" Ramazon is three years old and cries a lot; he sleeps during the day, and during the night, he stays awake and cries. My poor mother gets tired of carrying this boy.

Sometimes he tells her, "Take me to Usta bobo's house so he can give me almonds," and my poor mother takes him there. And the next day, he says he "wants to go to Islombeh" and "I want to eat dried cantaloupe" and "I want to eat sweets."

Ramazon usually increases his evening tours during the summer. One day, my sister, Sharifa, found a way to scare him. She went to the kitchen and came out, wearing a white robe. Ramazon was frightened and kept quiet.

The evening visits wearied my mother within a week. Unfortunately, Mulla Ramazon heard his mother and grandmother's whisperings and as soon as it was evening, he got a big stick and stood in front of the kitchen. My sister, Sharifa, couldn't get close to the kitchen, with the white robe in her hand and Mulla Ramazon being armed. "Oh white robe, come here!" my mother called. But the white robe couldn't get close to the kitchen to wear its robe and come out. The guard did not dare leave its position for fear of letting the white robe come out. "Maybe the white robe went to visit its aunt," my mother finally said. So, the crying Mulla defeated the white robe. At midnight, he insisted on going to his uncle Nizom's house and my mother carried him and took him to his uncle. Uncle Nizom filled Mulla's hat with raisins.

The evening of the next day, the journey to Kiyvony Bibi's house began. There were always pancakes at Bibi's house and Bibi gave some of them to Mulla and filled his handkerchief with sugar. On the way back, Mulla dropped his handkerchief and the sugar spilled on the sand. He started crying and demanded that my mother collect his sugar from the sand. Not knowing what to do, my mother muttered a few inexplicable words. At this moment, a huge, white thing appeared and started to approach them. Mulla Ramazon felt scared, but he licked the sand once or twice before running to his grandmother. "Grandma, the white robe has returned from its aunt's house," he told her. After this incident, Mulla Ramazon's evening journeys and adventures were over. My mother says that what they saw was a jinn but God only knows what they saw!

Mulla Ramazon had a lot of habits. Inside a newly bought chest, my mother kept sweets and chocolates wrapped inside a towel. She set the table with these sweets whenever there were guests at the house. The other day, my mother opened the chest and found that the towel was empty; she could find neither the sweets nor the chocolates. "Who could open the heavy lid of this chest?" my mother wondered and then smiled, because she noticed that there was a staple missing. "Mulla Ramazon has eaten all the sweets and chocolates," she thought to herself.

My mother did not say anything; instead she set the table in the guest room with raisins, dried apricots, and other fruits. Suddenly, she heard a little boy crying; it was undoubtedly Ramazon. He was lying down in the hall, under the big terrace and crying, "My sweets, my sweets." This little boy had hidden a big sugar cube in his pants and when he had entered the bathroom, the sugar cube fell into the toilet! This was the cause for everyone's laughter! Later that day, Ramazon's grandfather, Mulla Rajab came, bringing a lot of sweets, and he gave them to Ramazon.

Ramazon grew up and became a well-to-do-man. My sister's husband, Ramazon's father, always used to tease him and tell him, "Hey, chocolate-lover! I will marry you to Boqi Haluji's daughter!"

However, Ramazon did not marry Boqi Haluji's daughter; he married Hursindoy, the shepherd's daughter. Hursindoy had beautiful eyes and thick hair that covered her shoulders.

Whoever would look at Ramazon's house would surely admire it. His table was constantly full of sweets and chocolates. If he ever went to visit one of his friends, Ramazon never forgot to take lots of sweets with him because little children always surrounded him and said, "Uncle Ramazon, give us some sweets!"

And there were always sweets in Uncle Ramazon's pockets!

The Sensitive Case

By Farhod Musajonov

Several years ago, a famous comic actor showed up in the office of the theater manager. After exchanging greetings, the comedian raised the issue that he had come for. "I came with a suggestion," he said. "My suggestion is to organize a small group on the stage that you will supervise. In this group, we will organize satires and spoofs, criticize a few faults of some people, and laugh at these faults."

The manager looked at the comedian for a long time as if to say, "You idiot, you came to me with this suggestion? And is this what you call a suggestion?" The comic actor sat with patience and tolerated the manager's look. "Okay, your suggestion is not a bad one," finally replied the manager. "But if we think deeply about this issue, the case has a sensitive side to it. It's true that our lives are not faultless, because we do commit mistakes. But does it make sense to expose these little mistakes and annoy people? Our job is to encourage people to do great work. Of course, laughing—specifically, inoffensive laughing—is an essential thing but is it necessary to expose faults in order to produce laughter? Isn't there any other way for us to laugh? Is it necessary to laugh at faults?"

"Then, what do we laugh at?" asked the comedian, smiling.

"Laugh at anything you want. The most important thing is that you should not laugh at people's faults," answered the manager. He turned the conversation into a debate and continued, "Let's suppose, for example, that you get on the stage and laugh uproariously by yourself without any interruptions. The audience will also laugh because laughing is contagious."

"But isn't that just meaningless laughing?" asked the comedian.

The manager replied, "Don't think about meaning. We do not want meaning; we want laughter!"

"Is that so?" the comedian asked. "We can do what you said. But if we think about this deeply, this is a sensitive case."

"Excuse me?" asked the manager, agitated.

"No, there's no need to be upset about it," the comedian said, "but this case is a sensitive one. Okay, let's suppose that I get on stage and I laugh by myself without any reason, like you said. It's possible that some of the audience will laugh as well, because, like you said, laughing is contagious. But, what if a lot of the spectators think, 'Has the comedian gone crazy? Who allowed him to get on stage?' Maybe they'll say, 'The stage managers have taken no responsibility at all.' So, in the end, it still goes back to criticism. I say that in this situation, our talk goes back to criticism."

"If we do consider the issue from this angle, in truth, it does go back to criticizing. Hmmm . . . what if we do this? Let's assume that you get on the stage, acting solemn, trip over something, and fall on the floor. Then, everyone will laugh at you. Once I saw an acrobat doing the same thing at a circus and I laughed a lot," the manager said.

"Okay, we can do as you say," responded the comedian. "But if we think about this deeply, the case has a sensitive side."

"Excuse me?" the manager spat back again.

"No, no, don't be upset," said the comedian. "But the case is sensitive. Let's assume that I did fall on the floor on stage and maybe a couple of idiots will laugh at me. But other spectators will think differently. They might wonder, 'Why did he fall on the floor? Maybe there is a nail on the stage and they don't have maintenance to fix it. This means that the stage managers are irresponsible people.' In this situation, our talk goes back to criticizing."

The manager said, "If we think about the issue from this angle, we might indeed be criticizing. Okay then, this is what we'll do! Let's imagine that you get on stage, look at the audience, and frown without any reason."

"Did you also see this at the circus?" the comedian asked.

"Yes, I saw this at the circus," answered the manager.

"And did you laugh a lot?" the comedian asked again.

"Yes, I did," the manager replied.

"Okay, we can do as you say," the comedian said. "But if we think about this deeply, the case has another sensitive side."

"It does?" the manager said, visibly frustrated.

"No, there's no need to be upset," the comic actor said. "But this is a sensitive case. Let's imagine that I did frown without any reason, some of the audience might really laugh. As for the others, they might think, 'Why is this comedian frowning? He's afraid of laughing at faults that some people make in their lives until now; that's why he's frowning!' Won't they think like this? I say that in this situation, our talk still goes back to criticizing."

"If we do consider it from this point, we're still going back to criticizing; it's true," the manager replied. "Okay, then how can we produce laughter? Indeed, it's a very sensitive case!" Suddenly, the manager leaned forward and whispered in the comedian's ear, "Listen, don't think that I detest criticism. I'm not thinking about myself. As you know, different kinds of people attend the theater, and not all of them like criticism."

The comedian also leaned forward and whispered in the manager's ear, "There's something wrong with people who do not like criticism. For this reason, they hate it because they're afraid of being exposed!"

"Yes, well done!" answered the manager happily. "So, is it necessary for us to investigate simple faults in our radiant and prosperous lives?"

"Okay, then what do we do with people who sometimes commit faults in their lives?" asked the comedian.

"Never mind, my friend," replied the manager. "We'll strongly criticize those people who have faults in them. When their faults are exposed, yes, at that time, we'll strongly criticize them, without fear and mercy."

The comic actor looked at the manager in the face, smiled, and left the office. The manager doubted in his heart and followed the comedian hurriedly. "Stop! Why are you smiling?" asked the manager. This time, the comedian smiled even more widely. The manager got worried and asked him again, "Why are you smiling? And why is your face so red, as if it looks burnt?" The comedian, at hearing these words, couldn't help but laugh out loud. "Why are you laughing at me?" asked the manager, trembling.

"Human beings laugh whenever they want," answered the comedian. "Is laughing controllable?"

How I was a "Mister" for a Month!

by Sa'dulla Siyoyev

Last year, I became acquainted with a foreign young man called Charley Stefford. He is from Illinois of the United States. He had come to our country, intending to live in one of the Uzbek villages and to get to know our customs and traditions. One day, the mayor of the region, along with his assistants, brought this young man to my house and said, "Hikmatilla, this young man is our guest," pointing to Charley, "and he's a researcher. He wants to write a book about the history of Central Asia's inhabitants and about their lives today. I brought him to you, hoping that you'll allow him to be a guest at your house for a month. You're a generous man, and you have a big home and a big heart. Charley will not be a burden on you, for he'll take care of his own expenses. All I'm asking are your kind words and your answers to his questions. Is that okay?"

"Certainly," I replied, "My house is always open to guests. However, I have a condition."

"And what would that be?" asked the mayor, puzzled.

"My condition is that he shouldn't drink too much. I've heard that Americans drink liquor in excessive amounts. I do not like those who drink liquor."

The mayor laughed and said, "Okay, I'll tell him." He turned to the translator who said something to Charley in a foreign language. Charley, in turn, nodded his head and said, in English, "Yes, yes!"

And so, Charley settled in our home and I started calling him Charleyvoy. During the first week or so, we had a translator come to our home to explain to us each other's words. But then, gradually, we were no longer in need of a translator. Little by little, I started to understand English, and Charley started to understand Uzbek. If things got really bad, we conversed in sign language. For example, I brought my hand close to my mouth and touched my throat, and this meant, "Would you like some tea?" or I placed a spoon in a bowl and pointed to it and Charley would reply, in English, "Yes!" or "No, no!" moving his head, and from this, I would know what he meant.

It was *navroz*, which is also called the Persian New Year, during the time that Charley was staying at our place. "You're one lucky man, you'll get to see our folk holiday and eat sumalak[8]," I thought to myself. And as I expected, three days later, our next-door neighbor, Musharraf started cooking sumalak. Charley, of course, got his video camera ready, went near the pot, and started recording everything the women were doing right from before sunset. All of a sudden, he asked me in sign language, "What food is this?" Oh, God! How would I ever explain this to someone who does not understand the language? I thought for a while. Then I placed a handful of wheat on my palm, and on top of it, I put some grass. After that, I cut the

---

[8]   sumalak: an Uzbek food prepared in spring

grass with scissors and sprinkled flour on it. All the while, Charley was watching me with interested eyes.

"And this is how sumalak is prepared, my friend. Sumala-ak!" I told him. "Sum . . . Sum-malek," Charley repeated and immediately scribbled it down in his notebook. He sat with the women until dawn. He even tried imitating them moving the contents of the pot. Generally speaking, this was Charley's habit—he liked to touch, smell, and taste anything that he considered weird! One day, my wife was grinding grains and Charley came along, carrying his video camera. He looked at us for a while, then asked my wife to give him the pestle. My wife gave it to him, smiling. Charley lifted it up high and hit the mortar with it. The mortar tipped over and the grains scattered all over the ground. Charley's face immediately reddened and he bent his head down, apologetically. He squatted down and started gathering the scattered grains.

The other day, an interesting incident happened. Forty days ago, there came a new member into our family; we now have another grandchild. Our daughter-in-law's parents wanted to bring the cradle and as you know, cradle giving in the Uzbek culture, resembles a small ceremony. Having thought about that, I invited the English school-teacher, Manzura, because I did not want Charley bothering me with "What's this?" and "How's this?" questions.

Everything happened just as I had expected it—Charley recorded the whole event from the very beginning until the end. Even the decorated toy horse, along with my grandchild, became the hero of the evening, for he took pictures of it at least ten times. Finally, it was time for the cradle. Manzura explained the purpose of the cradle to Charley in detail. Suddenly, Charley's eyes fell upon the sumak[9]. He took it and started blowing in it as if it were a whistle. "What's this? It's a flute, right?" he asked.

"No, this isn't a flute; it's a kind of mini-sewerage system, specifically created for babies," Manzura tried explaining.

"Please demonstrate how this device is used," Charley insisted.

He was, after all, our guest, so I took him to our backyard and called one of my grandsons. I told him, "Ali, my son, kindly show to our guest how this sumak is used." At first, Ali just stood there, feeling shy, but then, he took some water and poured it into the sumak, showing it to Charley. "Ok, ok. Good, good!" Charley said, in English, happily. In short, I took another sumak from an old cradle and gave it to Charley. He thanked me twice for the gift, saying in English, "Thank you! Thank you!"

Eventually, I got tired of communicating with Charley in sign language, so I had Manzura come to our house every day. Together, we explained to Charley the meaning of the amulet worn to prevent the evil eye and the characteristics of the plow. We said that the container is the 'separator' and that the mortar is the grinder and so on.

---

[9] sumak: a pipe-like device that is used for carrying the baby's urine into a container

The other day, our neighbor's son, Sodiq was leaving to serve in the military army and so, we also went to bid him farewell. His mother gave him a loaf of bread to bite; then she hanged it on a niche. When Charley saw this, he asked me, "Why didn't she give him the bread? He could eat it on his way."

"Look," I told him, "his bag is full of food. As for the biting of the bread, it's a custom. It means that his mother wishes him to return back to the place where he bit the bread safe and sound." Charley wrote down everything I told him in his notebook. To make a long story short, during the whole month that he stayed with us, Charley recorded every single thing that seemed strange to him, and wrote down his observations.

As for me, I was a "mister" during that month. Because it was difficult for Charley to say 'Hikmatilla,' he called me 'Mr. Hek-matilda' instead. After exactly thirty days, the mayor of the province came once again. Again and again, Charley took pictures of my family members. He even hugged my 82-year-old mother goodbye. Before getting in the mayor's car and leaving, he repeatedly said, this time in Uzbek, "Thank you! Thank you!"

For two whole months, we did not hear anything from Charley. During mid-summer, I got a letter from him. He had sent his letter to the computer in the district's government office. After greeting and expressing his gratitude for being hosted well, he wrote as follows:

"Mister Hek-matilda! I lived a whole month at your home. I breathed from the same air you breathed. I observed your livelihood,

your everyday activities, your customs, your joys, your sorrows . . .
I tried analyzing them by myself, and I compared them to that of
others. I wanted to come up with a reasonable explanation, but no
matter how hard I tried, I couldn't. And I haven't understood the
Uzbeks completely. So, what kind of people are they? What is their
inner spirituality like? What are the roots of their hearts? What are
the characteristics of Uzbeks that differentiate them from other
nations? In short, who are you guys, Mr. Hek-matilda? I await your
response. Without your explanation of who the Uzbeks are, I will
not be able to find an answer to this puzzle. Regards, your friend,
Charley."

I sat and thought for a long while: indeed, who are we?
There is a famous poem called "My Uzbek" by Erkin Vohidov;
the poet tries to define who the Uzbek is, but can a single poem
contain the Uzbek's grandness? And what about me? How
will I squeeze the Uzbek lineage and ancestry into one letter?
Although I knew it was an impossible thing to do, I tried writing
the following letter:

"Hello, Charleyvoy! To be honest, my friend, your question,
'Who are the Uzbeks?' has really tired me. Charley, you know
Nasriddin Afandi, the hero of Uzbek folk tales, and you have read
and heard about his adventures, right? In brief, Nasriddin Afandi
is the symbol of Uzbeks. If you look at Nasriddin Afandi, then
you're looking at Uzbeks. At times, he is wise and all-knowing,
and at times, he is simple and stupid. Sometimes he is clever and
other times he is an imbecile; and there are times when he seems
the greediest but there are also times when he is the most generous

person. We, Uzbeks, are a nation who love guests. For it is an Uzbek who brings in a pot as big as himself, invites both those whom he knows and those whom he doesn't know, and throws a wedding party; and after the wedding is over, he pours water into the big pot, eats dried up bread, and remembers how he celebrated the party. In order to accomplish what we want, we address a person our son's age with extreme respect as if he were our older brother, for we are a nation that likes complimenting.

"And I don't think there is a nation that expresses affection more than we do and I will give you an example, Charley. Two friends are traveling. They are at the train station and the train has just arrived. Now they have to get in the train. One gives way to another, saying, 'After you,' but the other steps back, replying, 'No, no, after you.' The first one speaks again, 'It would be a shame if I got in before you. I have to respect you, therefore, you go in first.' Eventually, the train leaves and the two friends are still showing their affection and respect toward the other. These people are also Uzbeks!

"A man works by himself in his farm from the early morning until after sunset, then comes back home and only drinks green tea, giving thanks to God, and goes to sleep. This content man is also an Uzbek.

"Just yesterday, my neighbor, who had a low income, used to drink soup with no meat in it. But today, there appears to be some money in his pockets so he has become an arrogant person and has quite a big belly too. In the past, if he saw me, he used to say,

'Good morning, fellow neighbor,' but now, he says, 'How are you, my friend? I see you've lost weight,' feeling proud of himself. And he is also Uzbek. To tell you the truth, Charley, I myself do not recognize my nation sometimes! To make a long story short, let me tell you three things and from these, you can come to a conclusion:

"Several centuries before Columbus, my grandfather, Beruniy discovered the country that you are living in right now, and he even drew the map for it as well. This is one thing. The word medicine has been inherited from my grandfather, Ibn Sino. 'Madadi Sino' gradually changed to 'medicine.' As you know, Ibn Sino's books have been used as references in Europe for six hundred years and have been handed down from generation to generation. This is another thing.

"And finally, here we are in the era of computers and you have sent your letter to me through the internet. But have you ever thought about the person who first invented the algorithms? Yes, well done! Algebra and algorithm were both invented by my great grandfather, Musa Al-Khorazmiy. Since Europeans could not pronounce the word 'Al-Khorazmiy,' they changed it to 'algorithm.' So, here you go; this is the Uzbek, simple-hearted, who is sometimes active and other times lazy, and who sometimes works without stopping to rest. You have finally known how an Uzbek is like and what kinds of things he is able to do.

"There are different kinds of wishes in this world, but the 'Live long' or 'May you live a long life' wish is most commonly used by us, Uzbeks. For we do not say, 'May you live to be ninety or hundred,' but we say, 'May you live a long life!' And this is what I wish for you too, Charley. May God bestow on you a long life. Regards, your friend, Sa'dulla Siyoyev, on behalf of Hikmatilla."

Biographical Information

The Authors

Khayriddin Sultonov

He was born in Tashkent in 1956. He has published several books: "The Sun is for Everyone" (1980), "The Tale of the Evening" (1983), "My Mother's Country" (1987), "Life Passes" (1988), and "Bobur's Dreams" (1992). Sultonov has also translated some Russian writers' works to Uzbek: Y. Nagibin, S. Alekseyev, and F. Shukshin.

Ghafur Ghulom

(1903-1968) He was born in Tashkent. He published nearly twenty poetry collections, including "Live Songs," "Kokan," "You're not an Orphan," "Longing," and "There will also be Celebration in our Street." He was a member in the Academy of Sciences in Uzbekistan. He also worked in the following newspapers: "Kambag'ol Dehqon" (The Poor Farmer), "Qizil O'zbekiston" (The Red Uzbekistan), and "Sharq Haqiqati" (The Truth of the East).

Abdulla Qahhor

(1907-1968) He was born in Qoqon City in Fergana. He published a novel, "The Lamps of Qoshchinor" and numerous comic plays, including, "The Sick Teeth," "The Sound from the Coffin," and

"My Dear Mothers." He also published a number of stories: "Love" and "Stories from the Past." Qahhor translated Gorky's "My Universities," Gladkov's "The Horse with the Fire," and Tolstoy's "War and Peace" to Uzbek.

Said Ahmad

He was born in Tashkent in 1920. He has published a trilogy, "The Horizon," and several poetry collections, such as "Love," "Stories of Fergana," "Of Man-like Heart," and others. He became famous as a playwright; he has written numerous plays, including "The Brides' Revolution" (he wrote this based on his short story), "The Groom," and others. Ahmad translated some literary writings to Uzbek. His stories have been translated to different foreign languages as well.

Nargiza Ghulomova

She was born in Tashkent in 1965 and she graduated from the College of Biology and Soil Science in Tashkent University. She published her short stories in numerous international magazines and newspapers. Her short story collection, "The Meeting" was published in Ghafur Ghulom Publishing House in 2008.

Toghay Murod

(1948-2003) He was born in the province of Surkhandaryo. He has published several stories, such as "People in Moonlight," "Mother Earth's Song," and others; and a novel, "The Inherited Fields from my Father." He translated Jake London's stories and his play, "The Rich Man's Daughter" and E. Seton-Thompson's book, "The Wild

Horse." Murod also worked as the chief editor of "Fan va Turmish" (Science and Life) magazine.

Normurod Norqobulov

He was born in the province of Qashqadaryo in 1954. He served in the army between 1971 and 1973. He graduated from the College of Journalism in 1982 and is now working in Drama and Literary Programs Department in Uzbekistan TV.

Oydin Hojiyeva

She was born in Bukhara. She has published more than twenty poetry collections, such as "Songs that I Love," "The Morning Dew" (in Russian), and "The Flower of the Dream." She has also written a book called "I'm Looking for Springs," stories, and poems for children. Hojiyeva works as the chief editor in the children's magazine, "Ko'lxon" (The Flame).

Farhod Musajonov

Author, prose writer, playwright, scriptwriter. He was born in Tashkent in 1932. He has published nearly thirty short story collections, such as "Running After the Sun," "Don't Give up, Ali Qoluv," and "A Drop of Water from the Spring." He has written a number of stories, including "On Monday Morning after Breakfast," "I Miss my Garden's Street," "The Sword and the Saber," and others; plays, including "The White Dove," "In Search of Salvation," "I'm Under Your Command," among others. Musajonov is currently working in "Uzbek-Film" Cinema Company.

Sa'dulla Siyoyev

He was born in Qarnoq, Kazakhstan in 1939; he studied in Tashkent State University. He has published several short story collections, a novel, "Avaz," and a historical novel, "The Sacred Man from Turkistan." Siyoyev's stories have been translated to Russian, Kazakh, Kirghiz, and Tajik. Siyoyev has also translated Russian stories by M. Zoshchenko, A. Arkanov, and G. Gorin.

Made in the USA
San Bernardino, CA
21 September 2016